Cook Yourself THIN Faster

Cook Yourself THIN Faster

Have Your Cake and Eat It Too
with Over 75 New Recipes You Can Make in a Flash!

with Lauren Deen

PHOTOGRAPHS BY EVAN SUNG

voice

HYPERION NEW YORK

Food styling by Morgan Haas
Prop styling by Christopher White

Copyright © 2010 Lifetime Entertainment Services

Library of Congress Cataloging-in-Publication Data has been applied for.

ISBN: 978-1-4013-4138-1

Hyperion books are available for special promotions and premiums. For details contact the HarperCollins Special Markets Department in the New York office at 212-207-7528, fax 212-207-7222, or email spsales@harpercollins.com.

FIRST EDITION

10 9 8 7 6 5 4 3 2 1

Contents

Sides / Soups / Salads

Dessert

Acknowledgments

The inspiration for this book came in response to the enormous enthusiasm of all the readers and viewers of the first *Cook Yourself Thin* book and television series. Thousands of you clamored "More! More! More!," and this book is for you, created by a number of talented people whom we would like to thank.

Lauren Deen's creative and editorial vision led us through the first book and series, and continues here—thank you for your delicious recipes and tips, and for all of your wide-ranging talents. Anne Petito project-managed the entire book process with enormous enthusiasm, professionalism, and grace. Stephanie Lyness and Genevieve Ko-Sweet provided invaluable help with recipe development and testing, and got us to the finish line!

Special thanks to Evan Sung, who once again captured gorgeous pictures with his keen eye and inimitable calm manner. Morgan Haas skipped her honeymoon to continue the delectable food styling. Many thanks to Christopher White for the lovely prop styling, as well as his Texan charm. And a big thank-you to Adam Wayson, Eddie Roche, and Rhonda DeGarmo, who all lent a critical hand at our shoot.

An enormous thanks to the Tiger Aspect USA/IMG team for all of their incredible help and support: Christine Connor, executive producer, and Adam Steinman, VP of development. On the business affairs and legal end, thanks to Peter Devita, and many thanks to William DeMayo for his efforts with our shoot. From the Tiger Aspect UK team, who created and originated the show, special thanks to Andrew Zein, managing director; Jo McGrath; and Jenny Spearing.

It's been a privilege to have another opportunity to create a book with Hyperion, who indeed are the perfect partners. A very special thank-you to Ellen Archer, president, and Barbara Jones, Voice editorial director, and our fabulous editor, Sarah Landis.

At Lifetime Television, special thanks to Andrea Wong, JoAnn Alfano,

Jessica Samet, Sandy Varo, Julie Stern, Linda Rein, Beck Sloca, and Doug Strasnick.

Lauren Deen would also like to thank all of the guests who participated in the show and shared their stories here. You were the ones who did all the hard work! And a very special thank-you to her family—Anthony, Mathias, and Natasha—who often found themselves eating a slightly different version of the same dish night after night, and all of the Bank family for their various kitchens and comments, and for all of their love and support.

Introduction

Here's the most important thing you need to know:

This is not a diet book—we don't believe in dieting. We don't want to tell you what *not* to eat. This is a book filled with delicious food that we want you to cook and enjoy so you can have your cake and eat it too!

We don't want you to give up your "guilty pleasures"—we just want you to eat better versions of them, which we've created for you. Everything is designed to come together quickly and simply, with style and of course big flavor and great taste! There's no reason to feel guilty about these dishes, and they're nothing like rabbit food. A few clever changes and some smart swaps will have you whipping up everything from Pasta with Sausage and Cherry Tomatoes (page 97) to Shrimp Scampi (page 105) and impressive desserts like Mocha Mousse (page 166) in a flash.

These recipes are quick to prepare, and they don't require exotic ingredients or a trip to the health food store. We've cut the calories and the fat out of your favorite recipes, and added new dishes for you to experience and devour guilt-free—like Chilaquiles (page 21), Cod Saltimbocca (page 102), and Meringue Clouds (page 157).

Good food that's good for you—it's that simple! There's no need to look for a quick fix—it's all right here—so get ready to *Cook Yourself Thin Faster*!

What's It All About?

Eating is one of life's greatest pleasures—and we don't want to take that away from you! The problem starts when we think losing weight means that we have to deny ourselves everything that isn't a green vegetable and give up all our favorite foods (wave good-bye to chocolate). We make ourselves miserable until our cravings give way to temptation. Sure enough, suddenly the diet's a disaster and we're back on a vicious cycle of deprivation and cheating.

The great news is that we know there's another way. If you want to drop a jeans size for good, you just need to become calorie aware. The key to weight-loss success isn't a magic potion or only eating six raisins a day. It's simply knowing how many calories are in the foods you're eating and how many calories your body needs. In this book we've done the math for you with calorie and fat counts for each recipe. Our tips and ideas show you clever ways to cut calories so you can start losing weight right away. If that sounds too difficult, just turn to some of the success stories from our first book and television show to read the real testimonials from people who've done it!

This is not a diet manual or a nutritional guide. It's a cookbook. We really believe that if you want to lose weight for good, the only way is to cook yourself to your goal. After all, if you're the one doing the cooking, you're going to be in control: You'll be mixing great ingredients together in the pan, not pouring in extra fat, sugar, or salt to perk up the flavor. And when you're the chef, you can make sure you cook smart.

None of us wants to follow a diet that tells us we can't even look at a piece of bread. You really can eat what you want—you've just got to be clever and creative about it, and watch your portion sizes. That's why we're here to help. Love cheese on your pasta? Then look for a really strong Cheddar or real Parmesan, and you won't need to use as much. Want to have chocolate cake? Let's face it: Who doesn't! So preheat the oven for our indulgent Chocolate Volcano Cakes (page 147). *Cook Yourself Thin Faster* is all about showing you how small changes in the way you cook and shop can help you cut your calories.

What about the "quick and easy" bit? If cooking is going to be a regular part of your life, then you need to make sure that it never becomes a chore. Recipes that are delicious to eat but can fit into a busy life of work, family, and friends are essential. To help, we've even picked out recipes that are ultraquick for those of you who like to be in and out of the kitchen in less than twenty minutes—just look for the lightning bolt! Most of these recipes have very short prep times and don't require a laundry list of ingredients either.

Counting Your Calories

The most important thing to remember is that the only way to lose weight is to eat fewer calories than you use up. Once you are consuming fewer calories than your body uses, you will start to lose weight.

A calorie is a unit of measurement that tells you how much energy is in food. We need that energy to breathe and for our body to function, as well as to walk and to exercise, but if we eat more calories than we use up, then we store that energy as extra weight.

One pound of fat contains approximately 3,500 calories. So in order to lose a pound of fat a week, you need to reduce your calorie intake by around 3,500 calories a week. On a daily basis, this could mean cutting down 500 calories. Five hundred calories may sound like a lot, but just one midmorning croissant with butter and jam and a latte will take you over that amount, so cutting down might not be quite as hard as you think. To lose two pounds a week, you would need to reduce your intake by 1,000 calories a day.

Depending on your current intake, most women will lose weight at a healthy rate of one to two pounds a week on a calorie intake of 1,500 calories per day (for men, it should be about 1,800 calories per day). Consult with your doctor for your ideal calorie intake rate.

Once you know what you need to slash, you also need to know how to maintain your goal weight.

We use this equation:

your goal weight x 10 = the number of calories you can eat per day

How Are We Going to Do It?

Forget crash dieting. Those diets don't work and they're not good for you. You might lose weight to begin with, but then, when the diet becomes too much, you go back to your old eating habits and the weight comes right back on, often leaving you in a worse place than you were when you started.

Results might not be as dramatic as with crash diets, but making small, gradual changes to what you eat will drop those calories and allow you to change your eating habits for good. The real beauty of this is that slow, steady weight loss is more likely to be permanent, and the changes you make will stay with you for the rest of your life.

The Key: Your Food Diary

A food diary is the best way to get a sense of how many calories you are consuming each day. Be ready: You may be really surprised, even shocked. Things add up quickly.

The best way to see where changes can be made is to analyze what you're eating currently by writing down everything you eat (and we mean *everything*—the devil's in the details here) in your food diary. Being as truthful as you can is key. After a week, sit down and try to see if any patterns emerge. If you notice that you're always grabbing a mid-morning snack, perhaps your breakfast isn't hitting the spot. If you're munching chips after work, eating dinner a bit earlier might help, or grabbing a better snack may be the answer.

That's where *Cook Yourself Thin Faster* comes to the rescue. We've done the work for you, cutting the calories and slashing the fats from your favorites and providing some new dishes that are sure to become favorites. You'll be replacing your caloric recipes with our new dishes in no time.

Take a look at your food diary and see how many calories some of your "guilty pleasures" contain and you'll see that cutting 500 calories a day is easier than you think.

It gets easier when you see our great 100 Calories or Less Snack List (page 8). And if you add some exercise you'll be in better health and you'll burn more calories to help you lose more weight. Now that's being good to yourself!

And don't forget—once you start losing weight, don't give up the diary! Continuing with your food diary is a really great way to stay on track.

Five Big Changes You Can Make

After you've analyzed your eating patterns, there are five really important changes you can make.

1. Eat Regularly

We're sure you know this one already: Don't skip breakfast! Research has shown that adults who eat breakfast are less likely to be overweight than those who skip it. We have a whole chapter of great breakfast ideas—and variations so you won't become easily bored.

Stay on a schedule. Plan ahead so you eat at roughly the same time each day, because then you'll be less likely to think about food in between meals and to resort to those high-fat and high-sugar snacks. When you know you're going to be on the run, pack a few smart foods in your bag to help you eat at your planned times. And don't let yourself get to a crisis point. Even if you've managed not to give in to a sugar craving, when you eventually do get to eat a proper meal, you are more likely to overindulge because the craving has made you absolutely starving and your hunger will be controlling you.

2. Watch Your Portion Sizes

Beware big, value-saving portions at restaurants and while at home. Big portion sizes mean you may be doubling your calories, and that's no bargain! Know what a real portion looks like. If you don't know how big a portion should be, then start looking carefully when you cook the recipes in this book to know what a good portion size should look like.

Don't use trendy oversized plates or you'll pile on the food to fill up the space. A good trick is to overfill a smaller plate—you *can* fool the eye! A reasonable portion of food, nicely arranged on a plate, won't leave you feeling cheated and will make you feel indulged. Also, while we're discussing time spent at the table—slow down! Give your tummy a chance to let you know when it's full, and drink plenty of water with your meals.

3. Avoid High-Fat Snacks

With snacks, you need to think ahead, or you'll find yourself reaching for a muffin at the coffee shop or a bag of chips as soon as you're hungry. We're recommending you have two 100-calorie snacks a day, so have a go at some of our great recipes for homemade snacks and keep a supply of your favorite treats from the snack list below. Each one is about 100 calories.

COOK YOURSELF THIN FASTER SNACK LIST

100 CALORIES OR LESS

2 medium apples

1 small banana

1 low-calorie hot chocolate drink and a small vanilla wafer

1 small bag of reduced-fat chips

2 breadsticks and 1 tablespoon light soft cheese

3 rice cakes

1 small packet of licorice

1 small container low-fat fruit yogurt

1 small packet flavored mini rice cakes

1 Low-Fat Granola Bar (page 37)

4 chocolate kisses

1 small handful of dried apricots

18 small pretzels

1 hard-boiled egg

Small (5-ounce) glass of wine

1 tablespoon peanuts and 2 tablespoons dried cranberries

1 cup baby carrots and 2 tablespoons hummus

Starbucks tall skinny latte

1½ cups strawberries

2 light string cheese snacks

2 sheets of graham crackers

Chocolate milk (1 cup skim milk plus 1 tablespoon light chocolate syrup)

1 cup raspberries with 2 tablespoons plain nonfat yogurt and
    1 teaspoon honey

3 cups air-popped popcorn

10 peanut M&M's

2 egg whites scrambled over 1 slice whole wheat toast

1¼ ounces turkey jerky

Mini Blueberry Muffin (page 32)

10 baked low-fat tortilla chips and 3 tablespoons salsa

½ cantaloupe

1 cup vegetable juice and 2 ounces oven-roasted turkey breast

About ½ cup frozen yogurt

Half an English muffin with 1 teaspoon peanut butter

½ cup edamame

1 cup cherries

10 raw almonds

> **NOTE:** Brands vary, so always check the
> nutrition labels.

4. Eat Lots of Fruits and Vegetables

Fruits and vegetables are fabulous, filling foods, packed full of important nutrients. At the same time, they are usually low in calories. It's because of this that the recipes included in this book are loaded with these wonderful foods. Remember, five servings a day is ideal—and easy with our recipes. Other tips to get your five-a-day include:

- Keep fruit out in a bowl, and always have one packed to go on the run so when you're hungry, you can just grab a piece.
- Try adding just one more variety of vegetable to everything you're making. If you're making a chicken and lettuce sandwich, slice in a tomato as well. If you're making a chicken and mushroom pasta, stir in some fresh baby spinach or chopped frozen spinach at the end.
- When in the produce aisle, veer off your usual list and reach for something new. Try jicama and cut it up instead of peppers for dips

and salads. Try a new green, like kale or Swiss chard, and swap it in almost any recipe that calls for spinach. Many supermarkets provide cooking tips in the produce aisle too.

- Experiment with more exotic fruits, such as mangoes and kiwifruit, and have these as a snack instead of sweets, or add them to smoothies.
- Don't forget that dried and frozen fruits (in natural juices) also count as one of your five-a-day, as well as frozen and canned vegetables.

5. Don't Forget the Starchy Foods

We mean it. This plan is not about cutting out any sort of food from your life. It's about balance: eating more of certain foods and less of others. Yes, eat lots of fruits and vegetables, but you can also have *some* starchy foods, preferably whole grains, including bread, rice, potatoes, pasta, and breakfast cereals.

Very often people cut these foods out when trying to lose weight in the belief that they are fattening. Too much of any good thing is fattening. But making sure your diet includes starches that are high in fiber (such as whole grain or multigrain bread, whole grain breakfast cereals, brown rice, and whole wheat pasta) will help you feel full longer. Start your day with our Overnight Oatmeal (page 33) and compare your energy levels after your usual slice of white buttered toast!

But Wait, There's More . . .

6. Exercise

You knew we'd be mentioning this somewhere, didn't you?

Let's face it, some of us do, and some of us . . . well, really need to. The best way to think about exercise is not as a chore, but just something to build into your day and be a part of your life. Walk to work, buy yourself a bicycle, take up swimming again—it doesn't have to be all gyms and spandex, if that's what's been putting you off. If you build half an hour of moderate exercise into your daily routine, you'll start to feel the difference—not just physically but mentally too.

Exercise is the other side of the coin in the weight-loss formula. The calories you're eating give you the energy you need for physical activities, but if you don't do any, your body will store these extra calories as fat. These recipes show you how to consume fewer calories—but of course, you can also use more calories up. The best weight-loss plan of all is one where you balance the two. Try it—you deserve it!

> **NOTE:** It's important to remember that the calorie values on these pages are not intended for anyone whose calorie requirements may be different for medical or health reasons. For example, if you are under eighteen years old, breastfeeding, or pregnant, you should not start a calorie-controlled diet without consulting your doctor. Furthermore, these plans are not intended to replace any advice that has been provided by a qualified health professional. If you have any medical problems, it is best to seek advice from your doctor before embarking on a calorie-controlled diet.

Good luck—
and enjoy cooking yourself thin faster!

Success Stories

Cook Yourself Thin Faster wasn't dreamed up in a gadget-filled professional kitchen or written by an haute cuisine chef. It's the result of a real love of food, filled with recipes that help you make better choices and use clever swaps so you will change the way you eat, and lose weight or maintain your weight by eating simple but delicious food that you crave. The first *Cook Yourself Thin* cookbook and television series were incredibly successful—all the guests on our show lost weight, felt better about themselves, and made real changes in their lives. We thought you'd like to hear a bit more about their stories and learn some of their tips.

Kristen

BEFORE: Size 14   **AFTER:** Size 10

"I was saying, 'Hello, size 14—' Now I am a 10—<u>I am a 10!</u>"

Kristen was a self-proclaimed junk food junkie. She loved her burgers, fries, and a shake, her pizza with everything, and her drive-through breakfast sandwiches. And guess what—she still loves them all, but now they're CYT versions. Ask her how she dropped those two dress sizes, and this is what you'd hear:

"That (weight loss) was definitely, totally from 'cooking myself thin.' I followed the *CYT* way. I got healthier, low-calorie foods. And you know what? I realized that you are what you eat, so I got foods that were vibrant, that were firm—and that were just—they were colorful. So I am vibrant, firm, and colorful.

"I don't feel like I've lost anything. I don't feel like I'm sacrificing anything. What I was eating was making me feel heavy and sloppy. Like that breakfast sandwich—my breakfast sandwich was sloppy. Your breakfast sandwich was perky and cute and tasty. Guess what? I am what I eat!"

Has she slipped up?
"I have. I have slipped up, and you know what? My body was, like, 'What are you putting in me? Let's go back to that other good stuff.' So that's what I did."

Any advice for those who are still battling their diets?
"It's not hard, it's really not. It's just like, good food, bad food. Feel good, feel bad, the choice is yours. It can be done. You, too, can Cook Yourself Thin!"

Trisha

BEFORE: Size 12   **AFTER:** Size 8

This television news producer is always on the go—and was going to the refrigerator way too often to binge on cheese! After learning the CYT way, combined with a new exercise program, Trisha dropped two dress sizes in six weeks, and has continued to take off—and keep off—more than twenty pounds, and she's still losing!

"I feel great. I've worked really, really hard, but you know, I saw results, and when you see results, it's like, 'Wow, I can continue doing this.' I would've thought the weight would have come off more quickly. I'm losing about two pounds a week.

"I've changed my eating habits considerably. My nightly cheese and chorizo fest doesn't happen; I only drink one glass of wine a week now and have been eating a lot more vegetables.

"Turkey bacon—35 calories per slice—has become my savior. I find if I have two slices at about 11 A.M. every day, I can eat a reasonable lunch. I also reward myself every night with nonfat hot chocolate (around 50 calories) instead of a glass of wine to wind down my day.

"I haven't found cooking healthfully or making good food decisions on a daily basis all that difficult. In fact, it's been fun trying new recipes and surprising my friends with the substitutes I've made to make food more healthy.

"It's a mind-set more than a diet. It was fun to try to make food as yummy as I could without adding calories.

"I'm so excited . . . and you know, I feel confident and happy."

Trisha's Tips

- Spaghetti squash is a nice substitute for pasta (see Spaghetti Surprise, page 114).
- Swap nonfat yogurt if a recipe calls for sour cream.
- Planning what you are going to eat and choosing restaurants based on the menu is a good way to have a night out.
- Drink a lot more water and noncalorie drinks.
- Write down your activity and weight every day.
- Make it clear to your family and friends that you are trying to lose weight. I found my friends were INCREDIBLY supportive: They tried to set smart food out for me if they had a party, which helped; one would come with me to the gym; they supported that I wasn't drinking and didn't push me to imbibe.

A NOTE ABOUT OUR INGREDIENTS

All salt is kosher salt unless specified. We prefer the flavor of kosher salt, plus one teaspoon has 110mg less sodium than the usual table salt.

All butter is unsalted.

All eggs are large.

We prefer freshly ground pepper.

All cocoa powder is Dutch processed and unsweetened.

Whole wheat pasta is a healthy choice.

Eggs Italian Style, page 22

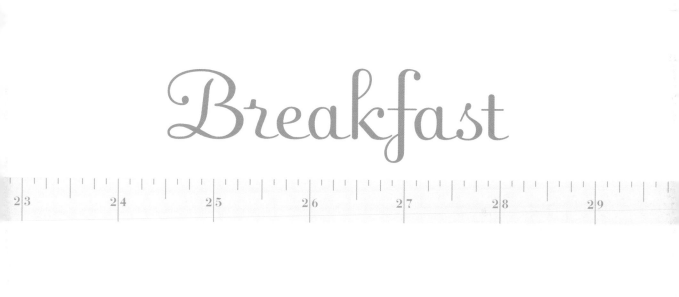

Breakfast

This is one of those times your mother was right. Breakfast is the most important meal of the day and should never be skipped.

You might think you're saving your 300 calories for later, but the mid-morning Danish and grande latte that you'll end up craving will set you back almost twice that. Instead, try eating our healthy delights and slow-release carb recipes for breakfast to help keep your blood sugar levels steady until lunch.

Start your day the *Cook Yourself Thin* way and you'll be well on your way to dropping that dress size!

Breakfast Burrito

Burritos are perfect for breakfast on the run or for days when you really need to get a good start. Using canned chiles keeps the eggs moist and cuts down on the need for more butter. For fancier presentation, slice them on an angle, place one half leaning alongside, and top with more salsa.

SERVES 4

NUTRITION PER SERVING:
CALORIES 320, TOTAL FAT 14g, SODIUM 722mg, SUGARS 2g

4   (8-inch) flour tortillas
2   large eggs
6   large egg whites
½   (4.25-ounce) can chopped green chiles
1   scallion, chopped
2   tablespoons coarsely chopped fresh cilantro
     Freshly ground black pepper
1   teaspoon unsalted butter
3   ounces turkey or chicken breakfast sausage links, chopped,
     or patties, crumbled
½   cup shredded low-fat Monterey Jack, Cheddar, or mixed
     "Mexican" cheeses
2   tablespoons jarred salsa, plus more for garnish if desired
     Hot sauce

1. PREHEAT THE OVEN to 350°F. Spread the tortillas over a baking sheet and set aside.

2. IN A BOWL, combine the eggs, egg whites, green chiles, scallion, cilantro, and a pinch of black pepper (the sausage provides enough salt). Whisk with a fork to blend.

(continued)

3. HEAT THE BUTTER in a medium nonstick skillet over medium heat. Add the sausage and cook, stirring, until cooked through, 2 to 3 minutes. Turn the heat to medium-low. Put the tortillas in the oven to warm. Add the egg mixture to the pan and cook, stirring often, until the eggs are set in large curds, 1½ to 2 minutes. Remove from the heat. Add the cheese and stir.

4. PLACE A WARM TORTILLA on each of 4 plates. Spoon the eggs in a line down the center of each tortilla. Add about ½ tablespoon salsa. Fold in the top and bottom, then roll in the sides. Serve immediately with hot sauce and top with more salsa if desired.

> TIP: To cut the fat content even more, omit the butter and replace with cooking spray.

Chilaquiles

Chilaquiles are a savory Mexican breakfast dish filled with vibrant flavors and contrasting textures—the soft scrambled eggs are cooked with chiles and crunchy tortilla chips and topped with cheese. The tomatoes keep the eggs nice and moist and replace the expected extra fat. These are crying out to be served with our Spicy Mary (page 41) for a fantastic brunch.

SERVES 4

NUTRITION PER SERVING:
CALORIES 110, TOTAL FAT 7g, SODIUM 159mg, SUGARS 1g

2   large eggs
2   large egg whites
1   teaspoon canola oil
1   tomato, cored, seeded, and diced
1   scallion, trimmed and thinly sliced
½   serrano chile, stemmed, seeded, and minced (or 1 jalapeño)
⅓   cup crushed baked tortilla chips
¼   cup shredded Monterey Jack cheese
     Salt and freshly ground pepper

LIGHTLY BEAT THE EGGS and egg whites together. Heat the oil in a 10-inch nonstick skillet over medium heat. Add the eggs and cook, stirring occasionally, until the eggs are partly set, about 1 minute. Add the tomato, scallion, chile, and chips. Cook, stirring occasionally, until the eggs are almost completely set. Season with salt and freshly ground pepper. Sprinkle the cheese on top, divide among 4 plates, and serve immediately.

Eggs Italian Style

This is a bold, flavorful twist on fried eggs and hash browns. Ready-made polenta stands in for the usual muffin or toast, adds a crunchy and creamy texture, and cooks up in an instant. Frying the tomatoes allows the natural sugars to caramelize. Breakfast Mediterranean style—just picture the Riviera!

SERVES 4

NUTRITION PER SERVING:
CALORIES 159, TOTAL FAT 9g, SODIUM 435mg, SUGARS 2g

1	tablespoon extra virgin olive oil
4	half-inch polenta slices (about 8 ounces total) from a ready-made polenta log (preferably Bel Aria brand)
8	half-inch tomato slices (or 8 plum tomatoes, quartered)
½	teaspoon salt
¼	teaspoon freshly ground pepper
2	teaspoons chopped fresh rosemary or oregano, or 1 teaspoon dried
4	large eggs

1. HEAT HALF THE OIL in a large nonstick pan over medium-high heat. Add the polenta and cook until crispy, about 1 minute per side. Transfer to a plate and keep warm. Add the tomato, and season with half the salt and pepper, and all of rosemary, and cook until the sugars in the tomatoes begin to slightly caramelize, about 30 seconds per side. Set aside and keep warm.

2. ADD THE REMAINING OIL to the pan and crack in the eggs. Season with the remaining salt and pepper, cover, and cook until the yolks are just set and the whites are opaque, about 2 minutes.

3. TO SERVE, place the polenta on each plate, top with 2 tomato slices, and slide an egg over the tomatoes. It won't be a perfect fit, so place the foods on an angle for a pretty presentation.

"Blintz" Pancakes with Blueberry Syrup

These pancakes are half the work and almost half the calories of cheese blintzes. Plus there's no need to take the extra step of making and filling the blintzes, as the egg whites make these light and fluffy with a golden crust. The protein from the cottage cheese kicks up your energy to start your day. If you're in a rush, just mix the egg whites directly into the cheese mixture. The pancakes won't be as light but they will be ready faster.

MAKES 8 SILVER DOLLAR PANCAKES
SERVES 4

NUTRITION PER SERVING:
CALORIES 250, TOTAL FAT 1g, SODIUM 467mg, SUGARS 22g

- ¾ cup low-fat (1%) cottage cheese
- ¾ cup fat-free sour cream
- ½ teaspoon vanilla extract
- ¼ teaspoon baking soda
- ¾ teaspoon baking powder
- ¾ cup all-purpose flour
  Pinch of salt
- 2 egg whites
- 2 teaspoons sugar
  Cooking spray
- ¼ cup pure maple syrup
- 1 cup blueberries

1. IN A MEDIUM BOWL, mix together the cottage cheese, sour cream, and vanilla.

2. IN A SMALL BOWL, mix the dry ingredients (except the sugar) and gently stir into the cheese mixture. Using a standing mixer fitted with a whisk or a handheld mixer, whisk the whites and sugar together until soft peaks form. They will have more than doubled in volume; do not overbeat

(continued)

or they will become dry. With a spatula mix in one third of the whites to lighten the cheese mixture and then gently fold in the rest of the whites.

3. SPRAY A LARGE GRIDDLE or nonstick pan with cooking spray and heat the pan over medium-high heat. Using a ¼-cup measure or large spoon, drop dollops of batter onto the hot pan and gently smooth to form silver dollar pancakes. Cook for 2 to 3 minutes until lightly golden brown and turn, cooking an additional 1 to 2 minutes until cooked through. Keep warm as you cook the remaining batter.

4. FOR THE SYRUP, combine the maple syrup and blueberries in a small saucepan and cook over low heat until the mixture is warm, stirring occasionally, about 2 to 3 minutes.

French Toast Bread Pudding

Ideal for brunch, this pudding is perfect for entertaining because you can make it the night before and wake up to a rich treat with half the calories of the usual French toast. For a pretty presentation, serve the squares with a dusting of confectioners' sugar and a few mixed berries.

SERVES 6

NUTRITION PER SERVING:
CALORIES 230, TOTAL FAT 6g, SODIUM 303mg, SUGARS 17g

	Cooking spray
4	cups (about 8 slices) whole wheat bread, cut into 1-inch cubes
4	ounces ⅓-less-fat cream cheese, softened
2	very ripe bananas, mashed
2	large eggs
2	egg whites
¾	cup lowfat (1%) milk
3	tablespoons pure maple syrup
½	teaspoon vanilla extract
	Zest of 1 orange
1	tablespoon confectioners' sugar, for garnish

1. LIGHTLY SPRAY an 8×8-inch baking dish with cooking spray.

2. ADD THE BREAD the bread to the pan. With a standing or handheld mixer, beat the cream cheese and bananas at medium speed until smooth. Add the eggs and egg whites, one at a time, mixing well after each addition. Pour in the milk, maple syrup, vanilla, and zest, and mix until smooth. Pour the cream cheese mixture over the top of the bread; cover and refrigerate overnight.

(continued)

3. PREHEAT THE OVEN to 375°F.

4. REMOVE THE BREAD MIXTURE from the refrigerator and let sit about 15 minutes. Bake for 30 to 40 minutes, or until a knife comes out clean and the center is set.

5. SIFT THE CONFECTIONERS' SUGAR over the pudding, cut into squares, and serve.

> NOTE: Serve with an additional tablespoon of maple syrup if desired, if you are not monitoring your sugar intake.

Asparagus and Goat Cheese Quiche

If you loved the mushroom and spinach quiche from our first *Cook Yourself Thin* cookbook, don't miss our latest version! We've cut the crust to lower the calories even more and kept the creamy custard. Swap the asparagus and goat cheese with your favorites—the varieties are endless—perhaps zucchini and Swiss, or Cheddar and sautéed bell peppers?

SERVES 4

NUTRITION PER SERVING:

CALORIES 103, TOTAL FAT 6g, SODIUM 249mg, SUGARS 3g

	Cooking spray
4	asparagus stalks, trimmed and cut into 1-inch lengths
2	large eggs
1	large egg white
¾	cup low-fat (1%) milk
¼	teaspoon salt
⅛	teaspoon pepper
2	ounces goat cheese

1. PREHEAT THE OVEN to 425°F. Spray four 5-ounce ramekins with cooking spray. Fill a large bowl with ice and cold water and set aside.

2. PLACE THE ASPARAGUS in a shallow dish with 2 tablespoons water, cover with vented plastic wrap, and microwave on High until bright green and just tender, about 3½ minutes. Carefully uncover (as the steam will be hot), place in ice bath to cool, and drain.

3. WHISK TOGETHER THE EGGS, egg white, milk, salt, and pepper until well blended. Divide the goat cheese and asparagus among the ramekins, and pour the egg mixture into the ramekins. Place the ramekins on a rimmed baking sheet.

4. BAKE UNTIL JUST SET (the center should still jiggle a little), about 15 minutes. Serve warm or cool.

Cheese Biscuits

Believe it or not, you can keep your beloved biscuits! A few smart swaps, like reduced-fat cream cheese and reduced-fat buttermilk, provide a rich yet light-textured biscuit. The pepper Jack gives it a nice kick, or you can use a milder Cheddar if you prefer.

MAKES 8 BISCUITS

NUTRITION PER BISCUIT:
CALORIES 155, TOTAL FAT 5g, SODIUM 616mg, SUGARS 2g

1⅔ cups all-purpose flour (use cake flour for lighter biscuits if possible), plus a few tablespoons more for forming
1 tablespoon baking powder
1 teaspoon baking soda
¾ teaspoon salt
¼ cup reduced-fat cream cheese, cut into small pieces, chilled
1 tablespoon unsalted butter, cut into small pieces, chilled
2 ounces low-fat pepper Jack or Cheddar cheese, grated
1 cup reduced-fat buttermilk

1. PREHEAT THE OVEN to 400°F.

2. LINE A LARGE BAKING SHEET with parchment paper or silicone mat.

3. IN THE BOWL of a food processor, combine the flour, baking powder, baking soda, and salt and pulse to combine. Add the cream cheese and butter and pulse until the dough looks like small peas.

4. TRANSFER THE MIXTURE to a large bowl and gently stir in the cheese and buttermilk, using a fork. The less you handle, the lighter the biscuit.

5. FORM THE DOUGH into a ball, place on a lightly floured surface, and smooth into a ½-inch-high round, gently patting with your hands. Cut out rounds with a 3-inch-diameter biscuit cutter and place on the prepared baking sheet. Gently press the dough scraps together and continue.

6. BAKE UNTIL THE TOPS are lightly browned, 10 to 15 minutes. Serve warm.

Mini Blueberry Muffins

Some mornings you just need a muffin, and these minis do the trick without packing on the pounds. The oats provide an energy boost and the orange juice cuts the amount of oil typically used in a breakfast muffin. Try raspberries or a mashed banana in place of the blueberries for your next batch. These freeze well if individually wrapped.

MAKES 12 MUFFINS

NUTRITION PER MUFFIN:
CALORIES 55, TOTAL FAT 2g, SODIUM 44mg, SUGARS 3g

¼ cup old-fashioned oats
¼ cup orange juice
1 large egg
1 tablespoon vegetable oil
½ cup all-purpose flour
2 tablespoons sugar
⅛ teaspoon baking powder
⅛ teaspoon baking soda
⅛ teaspoon salt
½ cup fresh or frozen blueberries

1. PREHEAT THE OVEN to 375°F. Line 12 cups of a mini muffin tin with paper liners.

2. COMBINE THE OATS and orange juice in a small bowl. In another small bowl, beat together the egg and oil. Whisk together the flour, sugar, baking powder, baking soda, and salt. Stir in the oat mixture until just combined. Stir in the egg mixture until well blended. Fold in the blueberries and divide among the muffin cups.

3. BAKE UNTIL GOLDEN and a toothpick inserted in the center of a muffin comes out clean, 10 to 12 minutes. Cool in the pan on a wire rack. Serve warm.

Overnight Oatmeal

Steel-cut oats, which are better for you than instant oatmeal, are a deeply satisfying and delicious way to begin your day. These oats have a nutty flavor and are packed with vitamins but usually take at least 30 minutes, leaving you standing and stirring over the stove. Our secret: Soak them overnight so they're ready in just over 5 minutes the following morning. This is a big batch so you have enough for your family or to stash in the fridge for a few days—just microwave with a bit more skim milk for a powerful breakfast.

SERVES 6

NUTRITION PER SERVING:
CALORIES 151, TOTAL FAT 2g, SODIUM 91mg, SUGARS 6g

3	cups water
1⅓	cups steel-cut oats, preferably McCann's
¼	teaspoon salt
2	tablespoons dried fruit (raisins, blueberries, or cherries) or ¼ cup fresh berries
¼	cup skim milk
2	tablespoons light brown sugar or pure maple syrup

1. COMBINE THE WATER and oats in a medium saucepan, cover, and leave out overnight.

2. IN THE MORNING, add the salt and bring the mixture to a boil. Partially cover and cook over medium heat for about 5 minutes, stirring frequently, until the oatmeal is creamy but still chewy. Add the dried or fresh fruit and milk for the last minute of cooking. Stir in the brown sugar or maple syrup and serve.

Violet Morning Smoothie

Feeling blue? This antioxidant boost will turn your morning around in a flash. Look for thick Greek nonfat yogurt to add a tangy flavor, or use your favorite flavor like vanilla or even blueberry for a richer flavor. Try freezing the pomegranate juice in an ice cube tray for a slushy treat.

SERVES 1

NUTRITION PER SERVING:
CALORIES 182, TOTAL FAT 1g, SODIUM 65mg, SUGARS 33g

⅓ cup pomegranate juice
¾ cup nonfat yogurt
¾ cup frozen blueberries
½ teaspoon honey

BLEND ALL THE INGREDIENTS in a blender until smooth.

> TIP: If you don't have frozen fruit, add 3 ice cubes.

Almondy Joy

Better for you than a candy bar, this creamy treat will get your day off to a supercharged start! Try swapping the vanilla yogurt for nonfat chocolate yogurt if you're still craving the candy bar taste!

SERVES 1

NUTRITION PER SERVING:
CALORIES 195, TOTAL FAT 2g, SODIUM 102mg, SUGARS 23g

⅔   cup nonfat vanilla yogurt
⅓   cup nonfat milk
1   teaspoon sliced toasted almonds
1   banana, cubed and frozen

BLEND ALL THE INGREDIENTS in a blender until smooth. Add a few tablespoons of cold water if the smoothie is too thick.

Low-Fat Granola Bars

Granola bars can be a girl's best friend or biggest nightmare if you don't read the label carefully, as they are often packed with fats and sugar. Making your own removes the mystery and lets you control your calories.

Try tossing in ¼ cup of chopped almonds or walnuts for a change. Just know that the fat and calorie count will increase, but these are good-for-you calories!

MAKES 8 BARS

NUTRITION PER BAR:
CALORIES 114, TOTAL FAT 1g, SODIUM 30mg, SUGARS 14g

Cooking spray
3   large egg whites, lightly beaten
¼   cup honey
1   teaspoon vanilla extract
½   teaspoon ground cinnamon
2   cups low-fat granola
¼   cup currants (you can use raisins too if you have them;
     if granola has dried fruit omit)

1. PREHEAT THE OVEN to 325°F. Lightly spray a 9-inch-square baking pan with cooking spray.

2. IN A SMALL BOWL, whisk together the egg whites, honey, vanilla, and cinnamon. Add granola and currants, and mix well. Lightly spray the bottom of a ⅓ cup measure with cooking spray and firmly press the measuring cup to flatten granola into the prepared pan.

3. BAKE UNTIL LIGHTLY BROWNED, 20 to 22 minutes. Place on a cooling rack and allow to cool completely in the pan for at least one hour. Use an offset spatula to trace around the outer edge and remove.

> TIP: This is a chewy granola bar. Omit the egg whites for a crunchy bar.

Stuffed Egg White Omelet

Egg-white omelets are how most of Hollywood starts their morning, and our version will leave you starstruck. Creamy goat cheese and fragrant herbs give the eggs a French flair, or start your day with our Tex-Mex version. Experiment with your favorite filling ideas—turkey bacon and low-fat Cheddar, perhaps? And don't skip the step of browning the butter; it gives the whites an added richness and deeper flavor.

SERVES 1

NUTRITION PER SERVING:
CALORIES 140, TOTAL FAT 9g, SODIUM 245mg, SUGARS 1g

3   large egg whites
1   tablespoon chopped fresh soft herbs (such as parsley, basil, dill, arugula, chives)
    Pinch of freshly ground black pepper
1   teaspoon unsalted butter
¾   ounce (about 2 tablespoons) crumbled fresh goat cheese

1. USING A FORK, whisk the whites with the herbs and pepper in a small bowl.

2. MELT THE BUTTER in a small (8-inch) nonstick skillet over medium-high heat. When the butter begins to turn golden brown and smells nutty, pour in the egg white mixture and cook, pulling the sides of the omelet in toward the center with a rubber spatula and tilting the pan to allow the uncooked egg to run to the sides, until the eggs are set, 30 to 40 seconds.

3. SPREAD THE GOAT CHEESE down the center third of the omelet. Use the spatula to fold the back third of the omelet in toward the center, then the front third. Let cook another 10 seconds to warm the cheese. Turn the omelet out onto a plate.

Variation: Tex Mex

SERVES 1

NUTRITION PER SERVING:
CALORIES 120, TOTAL FAT 6g, SODIUM 332mg, SUGARS 2g

1   teaspoon unsalted butter
¼   red or yellow bell pepper, cut into ⅓- to ½-inch dice
     Salt
3   egg whites
     Pepper
1   tablespoon shredded low-fat Jack or natural Mexican-style cheese

1. HEAT ½ TEASPOON of the butter in a small (8-inch) nonstick skillet over medium-low heat. Add the bell pepper and a pinch of salt and cook, covered, until softened and lightly browned, about 5 minutes.

2. MEANWHILE, whisk the whites in a bowl with a pinch each of salt and pepper. When the bell pepper is cooked, raise the heat to medium-high, add the remaining ½ teaspoon of butter, and cook until the butter is golden brown. Add the egg whites and cook as in the previous recipe, adding the cheese as before.

Spicy Mary

Wake up your brunch with this spicy drink. By omitting the olives, we've slashed more calories but kept the flavor by using celery salt on the rim, along with some snappy garnishes. To cut more calories, omit the vodka for a Virgin Mary.

SERVES 6

NUTRITION PER SERVING:
CALORIES 162, TOTAL FAT 1g, SODIUM 214mg, SUGARS 9g

	Zest and juice of 1 lemon
1	tablespoon prepared horseradish, drained
1	jalapeño pepper, minced
¼	teaspoon celery salt, plus more for garnish
3	cups ice
¾	cup vodka (or pepper vodka if preferred)
3	cups low-sodium tomato juice
1	tablespoon Worcestershire sauce

Garnish:
Lemon wedges
Celery stalks
Pickled jalapeño
Cherry tomatoes

1. PLACE THE LEMON ZEST AND JUICE, horseradish, jalapeño, and celery salt in the bottom of a pitcher and stir. Add the ice, vodka, tomato juice, and Worcestershire and stir to combine. (This can be mixed ahead without the ice and stored in the refrigerator for a few hours.)

2. TO GARNISH, prior to pouring drinks, trace a lemon wedge over the rim of a glass. Pour celery salt into a shallow bowl and twist the rim into the salt. Carefully fill the glass with ice and pour drink. Garnish with a celery stalk and drinks skewer or toothpick speared with a pickled jalapeño and a cherry tomato. Add a lemon wedge to the rim if desired.

Michele

BEFORE: Size 14   **AFTER:** Size 12; lost 7 pounds

Michele's wedding day was approaching, and the last thing she wanted was to squeeze herself into an unflattering wedding dress. She also wanted to create a new way to think about food for her new married life.

"The *CYT* experience for me was really a learning experience . . . it was a fun one and a little bit challenging. Overall, though, I would say that it was great. I became more conscious of my food choices—picking yogurt and maybe granola instead of chips and chocolate . . . I didn't eat as many cupcakes or cookies, too. I definitely thought twice about it when I came across them, and I only ate them once or twice during my six weeks. I realized that I had the self-control to make the right choices and really just take control of my food choices instead of letting the food and hunger or desire to eat something take over me!

"I tried new recipes from the cookbook, and I found that by making some small changes to healthier ingredients the food was still delicious and easy to prepare. I cooked more and that felt really great, knowing exactly what ingredients I was using and knowing that I was preparing something healthy and homemade for my fiancé and me to eat.

"I always make sure I have bananas or apples on hand, and even fruit cups are a healthy and quick snack when I'm feeling hungry. These and yogurt have really been my go-to foods instead of picking up a bag of chips or a cookie. They're really quick and easy snacks, and though people told me about them before, I always kind of put it off. Now if I don't have fruit, a fruit cup, or yogurt around I feel like I have nothing to eat! Haha!

"It's little things and baby steps that can bring you where you want to be. I feel better and I have more confidence in the way I look. I wake up in the morning, and instead of feeling like I have nothing to wear because my clothes are too tight, I feel like I don't have anything to wear because my clothes are too loose! That really is a great feeling, and it's a great reward for making a few changes. Nothing happens overnight, and as long as you stick with it and keep focused everything will be great—you'll look great and feel great!"

Hot Wings, page 57

Starters

Ah, crispy, salty, rich treats to start your meal, or to serve alongside drinks— all the delectable bits that diets deny you!

Well, we've created lighter but stylish bites of all shapes and sizes so you won't feel deprived—and don't miss our Blush Sangria or Pineapple Mojitos!

Cheers!

Stuffed Mushrooms

An international hors d'oeuvre that's fast and fabulous without the added fat! Japanese panko bread crumbs provide the crunch, and Italian Parmesan adds richness. The olive oil replaces the usual stick of butter, and we promise you, you won't miss it. These freeze well after baking, so make a double batch and gently rewarm in a low oven straight from the freezer.

SERVES 4

NUTRITION PER SERVING:
CALORIES 63, TOTAL FAT 4g, SODIUM 151mg, SUGARS 2g

1	box (10 ounces) white mushrooms, cleaned
4	scallions, trimmed and thinly sliced
1	tablespoon olive oil
¼	teaspoon salt
¼	teaspoon pepper
2	tablespoons panko bread crumbs
1	tablespoon freshly grated Parmesan cheese

1. PREHEAT THE OVEN to 400°F. Line a large rimmed baking sheet with aluminum foil.

2. POP THE STEMS off the mushrooms and chop; arrange the mushroom caps in a single layer on the prepared pan. Reserve 2 tablespoons of scallions for garnish. Heat the oil in a large skillet over medium-high heat. Add the scallions and cook, stirring, until fragrant, about 1 minute. Add the chopped mushroom stems, salt, and pepper, and cook, stirring, until tender, about 5 minutes. Remove from the heat and cool slightly.

3. DIVIDE THE MUSHROOM STEM MIXTURE among the mushroom caps. Combine the panko and Parmesan and press the crumbs gently into the mushroom stem mixture. Bake until the mushrooms are tender and the topping is golden brown, about 30 minutes. Garnish with the reserved scallions and serve.

Spinach Dip

Spinach dip seems like it should be good for you, but it is often filled with hidden fats. We've created a luscious version with nonfat yogurt and frozen spinach that comes together in a flash. Buy precut veggies and baked pita chips for an indulgent snack with less than half the usual fat and calories!

SERVES 4

NUTRITION PER SERVING:
CALORIES 53, TOTAL FAT 2g, SODIUM 301mg, SUGARS 5g

1	(10-ounce) package frozen chopped spinach leaves, defrosted
1	cup nonfat plain Greek-style yogurt
1	scallion, chopped
1	tablespoon fresh lemon juice
1½	teaspoons chopped fresh dill
½	teaspoon salt
	Pinch of ground red pepper
1½	teaspoons extra virgin olive oil

SQUEEZE OUT any extra water from the spinach with your hands. Measure out ½ cup of spinach and transfer to a mixing bowl. (Cover and refrigerate the remainder for another use.) Add the yogurt, half the chopped scallion, the lemon juice, dill, and salt and stir well to blend. Scrape out into a serving bowl. Sprinkle with the red pepper and drizzle with the olive oil. Serve with pita chips, toasted wedges of pita, or veggies.

> **NOTE:** Toss the leftover spinach into chicken stock for a quick soup, or your usual pasta sauce.

Blush Sangria

Sangria is a refreshing and gorgeous way to celebrate, and this rosé version is especially beautiful. Switch to green apples when peaches aren't in season, and try substituting a bottle of merlot or chardonnay for a lovely variation. If you don't have superfine or bar sugar, simply stir granulated sugar into a bit of very hot water until dissolved. The club soda splash cuts the calories by reducing the amount of wine you'd usually add.

SERVES 6

NUTRITION PER SERVING:
CALORIES 131, TOTAL FAT less than 1g, SODIUM 15mg, SUGARS 11g

1	bottle rosé wine, chilled
1	peach, thinly sliced
1	orange, halved and thinly sliced
½	pint fresh raspberries
2	tablespoons superfine sugar
	Fresh mint leaves, for garnish
1	cup club soda, chilled

COMBINE THE WINE, fruit, and sugar in a pitcher. Refrigerate for at least 20 minutes and up to a day. Serve over ice, garnish with mint, and top with a few splashes of club soda.

Roasted Chickpeas with Rosemary

These are addictive, packed with protein, and a surprising change from the usual fattening bar nuts. Play with the seasonings and lower the calories by swapping the rosemary and Parmesan for a tablespoon of curry powder or chili powder before baking.

SERVES 6 AS A SNACK
MAKES ABOUT 2 CUPS

NUTRITION PER SERVING:
CALORIES 217, TOTAL FAT 7g, SODIUM 610mg, SUGARS 7g

2   (15-ounce) cans chickpeas (sometimes labeled garbanzos)
2   tablespoons olive oil
½   teaspoon salt
⅛   teaspoon freshly ground black pepper or hot pepper flakes
1   tablespoon chopped fresh rosemary, or 1½ teaspoons dried
2   tablespoons freshly grated Parmigiano-Reggiano cheese
    Fresh rosemary sprigs, for garnish

1. PREHEAT THE OVEN to 400°F.

2. LINE A LARGE rimmed baking sheet with aluminum foil.

3. RINSE THE BEANS in a colander and drain. Gently rub the beans to loosen the skins. Discard the skins. (Don't worry if you miss a few.) Pat the beans dry with a towel and place in a bowl.

4. ADD THE OIL, salt, and pepper to the beans and toss to coat the beans evenly.

(continued)

5. SPREAD THE BEANS in an even layer on the baking sheet, place in a preheated oven, and bake for 30 minutes, until crunchy, stirring and shaking the pan midway through baking.

6. SPRINKLE THE HERBS evenly over the beans, and continue to cook for 8 to 10 minutes, until the beans are crunchy. Some will be slightly soft in the center.

7. REMOVE THE PAN from the oven and transfer the beans to a serving bowl. Sprinkle the cheese over the beans and stir.

> **NOTES:** You can easily double or even triple the recipe. Just make certain to use a second pan. The beans can be made ahead; wrap them tightly in foil and refrigerate. Reheat in a hot oven until crispy; sprinkle the cheese over right before serving.

Spanakopita

Greek spinach pies are usually made by brushing melted butter between layers of phyllo dough. We've cut out more than half the fat by replacing the butter with olive oil spray. Don't forget the mint; it adds a lovely nuance to the filling. These freeze beautifully and can become a main course for supper when served alongside soup or salad.

SERVES 4

NUTRITION PER SERVING:
CALORIES 117, TOTAL FAT 4g, SODIUM 381mg, SUGARS less than 1g

	Olive oil cooking spray
2	bags (6 ounces each) baby spinach
¼	cup finely chopped fresh mint leaves
2	ounces feta cheese, crumbled (about ½ cup)
⅛	teaspoon salt
¼	teaspoon pepper
4	phyllo sheets (17 × 12 inches each), thawed

1. PREHEAT THE OVEN to 375°F. Coat a 9×5-inch loaf pan with cooking spray.

2. COAT A 12-INCH SKILLET with cooking spray and heat the pan over medium-high heat. Add the spinach and cook, stirring, until just wilted, about 2 minutes. Transfer to a large bowl and cool slightly, about 10 minutes. Stir in the mint, feta, salt, and pepper.

3. FOLD EACH PHYLLO SHEET in half. Place one folded sheet in the prepared pan, pressing against the bottom and up the sides, and coat with cooking spray. Place one third of the spinach mixture in the pan and spread in an even layer. Repeat the layering two more times, coating each phyllo sheet with cooking spray.

4. BAKE UNTIL GOLDEN BROWN, 20 to 25 minutes, then transfer to a rack to cool slightly. Cut into 4 pieces and serve.

Hot Wings

If you loved the Buffalo Chicken Salad from the first *Cook Yourself Thin* book, you won't want to miss our version of this classic dish. Hot wings are usually fried and then sautéed in a buttery sauce. We've reduced the fat by baking the wings, though these are fantastic on the grill too! And of course, we lowered the fat from the dip for you too.

SERVES 4

NUTRITION PER SERVING, WINGS:
CALORIES 352, TOTAL FAT 24g, SODIUM 480mg, SUGARS 4g

NUTRITION PER SERVING, SAUCE:
CALORIES 23, TOTAL FAT 1g, SODIUM 73mg, SUGARS 2g

¼   cup plain nonfat yogurt
1   tablespoon crumbled blue cheese
½   teaspoon fresh lemon juice
¼   teaspoon pepper
12 chicken wings, wings and drumettes separated
¼   cup Buffalo hot sauce, preferably Frank's
1   tablespoon honey
1   teaspoon unsalted butter
4   celery stalks, cut into 3-inch lengths

1. COMBINE THE YOGURT, blue cheese, lemon juice, and pepper in a small bowl. Cover with plastic wrap and refrigerate until ready to serve.

2. PREHEAT THE OVEN to 425°F. Line a large rimmed baking sheet with aluminum foil. Arrange the wings in a single layer on the prepared pan and roast, turning over once, until cooked through, about 35 minutes.

3. MEANWHILE, combine the hot sauce, honey, and butter in a large bowl. Remove the wings from the oven and immediately transfer to the hot sauce mixture. Toss continually until evenly coated. Serve with celery and reserved blue cheese sauce.

Sautéed Corn Cakes with Smoked Salmon

This is the *CYT* take on beloved corn fritters, which are filled with added sugar and fat from frying. We've given them a more modern and healthier makeover—they're accented with smoked salmon and topped with a red onion and tomato salad.

SERVES 4

NUTRITION PER SERVING:
CALORIES 156, TOTAL FAT 5g, SODIUM 447mg, SUGARS 6g

2	cups corn, defrosted if frozen
2	tablespoons minced chives
2	teaspoons all-purpose flour
2	egg whites, beaten
1	teaspoon olive oil
⅓	cup reduced-fat sour cream
4	thin slices smoked salmon, about ½ ounce per serving
1	tomato, sliced
1	small red onion, very thinly sliced
1	tablespoon fresh lemon juice
¼	teaspoon salt
¼	teaspoon pepper

1. ROUGHLY CHOP 1 cup of the corn and place in a large mixing bowl. Add the remaining corn, the chives, the flour, and the egg whites. Mix well to evenly combine.

(continued)

2. HEAT THE OIL in a nonstick skillet over medium heat. Using a quarter cup measure, drop dollops of corn mixture into the pan. Cook until golden brown and crisp on the bottom, about 3 to 4 minutes. Flip carefully and cook until browned, about 2 to 3 minutes.

3. PLACE ONTO A SERVING PLATE and garnish with the sour cream, the salmon, and the tomato and onion slices. Sprinkle with lemon juice, salt, and pepper.

Pineapple Mojitos

This minty cocktail has an easy and tropical shortcut—just add a splash of pineapple juice instead of the traditional simple syrup and you have a festive drink that will transport you poolside in no time! Gently crushing the mint releases all the fragrance and flavor into the pitcher. Omit the rum for a new nonalcoholic refreshing family favorite.

SERVES 4

NUTRITION PER SERVING:
CALORIES 185, TOTAL FAT less than 1g, SODIUM 11mg, SUGARS 9g

¼	cup fresh mint leaves, plus sprigs for garnish
1	tablespoon light brown sugar
2	limes, cut into wedges, plus more for garnish
1	cup pineapple juice
1	cup white rum
½	cup club soda

USING A WOODEN SPOON, gently pound the mint leaves, sugar, and lime wedges in the bottom of a large pitcher to release the juice and dissolve the sugar. (Add a tablespoon of very hot water to help dissolve the sugar.) Add 3 cups of ice, the pineapple juice, and rum. Top off with club soda to taste. Pour into glasses over ice and serve. Garnish each glass with a lime wedge and mint sprigs, if desired.

White Pizza with Roasted Mushrooms

Don't skip this recipe—really!!! Want to know what to serve with cocktails or with a salad for a light dinner? This addictive pizza defines simple, sophisticated fare. It's so fast, so easy, and so delectable. Play with the herbs—try rosemary, thyme, or fresh or dried oregano. Swap the shiitakes for chopped portobellos, creminis, or even white buttons. Please make sure to buy Pecorino; it adds a lovely bite.

SERVES 8 OR 12 FOR STARTERS

NUTRITION PER SERVING:
CALORIES 160, TOTAL FAT 9g, SODIUM 212mg, SUGARS less than 1g

3	tablespoons olive oil
½	pound store-bought pizza dough
1	cup reduced-fat ricotta cheese
3	tablespoons grated Pecorino Romano cheese
	Freshly ground pepper
5	ounces shiitake mushrooms, stems removed
¼	teaspoon fresh sage, thinly sliced into ribbons
	Pinch of salt

1. PREHEAT THE OVEN to 450°F. Oil a 17×11-inch rimmed baking pan with 1 tablespoon of olive oil.

2. STRETCH THE DOUGH directly onto the baking pan, pressing and gently stretching to fill as much of the pan as possible. (It will not fill the entire pan.) Brush with 1 tablespoon of olive oil over the surface of the dough.

3. SPREAD THE RICOTTA CHEESE over the pizza. Sprinkle the ricotta with the Pecorino and pepper.

(continued)

4. TEAR THE MUSHROOM CAPS into small pieces and place in a small bowl. Toss with the remaining tablespoon of olive oil, the sage, pinch of salt, and pepper. Scatter the mushrooms over the top of the cheese.

5. PLACE IN THE OVEN and bake for about 15 to 20 minutes, until the crust is fully baked, and transfer to a cooling rack. Cut into slices (kitchen scissors work best) and serve immediately.

> **NOTE:** To check for doneness, remove tray from oven and slide a large spatula under center of pie. Crust should be fully cooked.

Pizza with Sweet Peppers and Goat Cheese

Once you've tasted these tangy-sweet peppers you'll be using them for everything—whizzing them for dips, tossing them with pasta, layering them in sandwiches, or using them as we do here, for a fast pizza topping. The best part is they can be made ahead and stashed in the refrigerator for a few days.

SERVES 8 OR 12 FOR STARTERS

NUTRITION PER SERVING:
CALORIES 157, TOTAL FAT 8g, SODIUM 308mg, SUGARS 6g

	Olive oil cooking spray
1½	tablespoons extra virgin olive oil
½	medium-sized white onion, quartered and thinly sliced
2	(10-ounce) jars (about 2 cups) drained roasted peppers, thinly sliced (packed in water, not oil)
3	tablespoons sugar
1	tablespoon sherry vinegar, preferably aged, or best-quality red wine vinegar
1	tablespoon water
	Coarse salt (kosher or sea)
½	pound store-bought pizza dough
¼	pound goat cheese, crumbled

1. PREHEAT THE OVEN to 450°F. Spray a 17×11-inch rimmed baking sheet with olive oil spray.

2. HEAT THE OLIVE OIL in a large skillet over medium-low heat. Add the onion and cook until softened but not browned, 5 to 7 minutes, stirring occasionally. Add the roasted peppers and cook for about 5 minutes, stirring. Add the sugar, vinegar, and water and stir until the sugar dissolves. Reduce the heat to low, and cook until the liquid is reduced, about 5 to 7 minutes, stirring occasionally. Season with salt to taste and let the pepper mixture cool slightly. (This can be made a few days ahead and kept refrigerated.)

(continued)

3. STRETCH THE DOUGH directly onto the baking pan, pressing and gently stretching to fill as much of the pan as possible. Spread the pepper filling evenly over the dough, place in the oven, and bake for 10 minutes. Rotate the pan, crumble the goat cheese over the surface of the pizza, and continue to bake for an additional 7 to 10 minutes, until the center of the pie is fully cooked. (Check by lifting the bottom of the pie with a large metal spatula.)

4. REMOVE FROM THE OVEN and transfer to a cooling rack. Cut into slices (kitchen scissors work best) and serve.

Seven-Layer Dip

We've slashed more than half the fat from this party favorite! Using canned black bean soup means there's no need to blend the beans either. This is served warm with baked tortilla chips for dipping. For a cool contrast, try serving jicama sticks too.

SERVES 8

NUTRITION PER SERVING:
CALORIES 236, TOTAL FAT 9g, SODIUM 743mg, SUGARS 5g

1	(15-ounce) can black bean soup, preferably Goya
2	avocados, peeled and seeded
2	tablespoons fresh lime juice
	Salt
5	tablespoons roughly chopped fresh cilantro
1	cup nonfat plain yogurt
½	cup low-fat sour cream
½	teaspoon chile powder
1	can roasted chopped green chiles, drained
1	(2.25-ounce) can sliced black olives, drained
2	cups fresh salsa
⅔	cup shredded low-fat Mexican 4-cheese blend or Cheddar cheese
2	scallions, chopped
	Low-fat baked tortilla chips
	Jicama sticks, if desired

1. SPREAD THE SOUP over the bottom of an 8×8-inch baking dish with a rubber spatula.

2. IN A BOWL, mash the avocados with the lime juice, ⅛ teaspoon salt, and 3 tablespoons of chopped cilantro. Spread over the soup with the spatula.

(continued)

3. IN THE SAME BOWL, stir together the yogurt, sour cream, chile powder, and a pinch of salt; spread over the avocado. Spread with the chopped chiles. Sprinkle with the olives. Spread with the salsa. Sprinkle the cheese over the top.

4. PREHEAT THE BROILER and arrange the oven rack about 4 inches from the heat. Broil to melt the cheese, 2 to 4 minutes. Sprinkle with the remaining 2 tablespoons cilantro and the scallions. Serve with baked tortilla chips and jicama sticks.

Carleen

BEFORE: Size 12   **AFTER:** Size 8; lost 14 pounds

Carleen is an inspiration—she was looking for a new job and struggling with the endless snacking that unemployment can bring, and she was also looking for some new romance in her life. Her dedication and generosity are awesome—she sent us an enormous "thank you" fruit basket, which we happily devoured!

"I want to thank you for allowing me to be a part of *Cook Yourself Thin*. This experience was one of the most exciting and rewarding experiences I have ever had. Not only did I drop the pounds needed, but I lost 2 whole dress sizes as well. I accomplished a goal that I set out to do. I have not only changed my life by eating healthier, but I will also continue to cook healthfully in all my meals.

"The best tip I think I learned was to eat in smaller portions and not eat until I'm exhaustingly full. I've learned to eat just to eliminate the hunger pain. I have shared your recipes with many friends. So many were impressed with my new look that they've made the decision to cook the meals to try to lose the weight themselves! I think it will happen if they stick to the recipes and exercise, just walking thirty minutes a day. If they have to snack, they need to make sure it's something that's low in calories. Eating a lot of fiber and whole grains is a plus.

"The key is not to give up, stay on track, believe, and keep the faith, and it will happen.

"*CYT* has made me a much happier person. I'm feeling confident, I'm feeling great about myself. I am just so overwhelmed with happiness right now, it's really changing my life. Thank you all so much. I am ecstatic with my life!"

Pasta with Sausage and Cherry Tomatoes, page 97

Mains

Comfort food, fast weeknight suppers, what to serve to a crowd, what to eat when you're really, really hungry—it's all here, without the usual fat and calories!

Whether you crave a hearty, filling main course or a quick light supper, we've created standout dishes that come together quickly and easily to feed you, your family, and your friends!

Chicken Cordon Bleu

A gourmet dish without all the fuss and fat, this old-school favorite gets a calorie cut. Go around the globe with your own variations—go Greek with feta, olives, and roasted peppers or try turkey bacon and pepper Jack for a Mexican twist.

SERVES 4

NUTRITION PER SERVING:

CALORIES 330, TOTAL FAT 12g, SODIUM 752mg, SUGARS 1g

4   boneless, skinless chicken breasts (about 1½ pounds total)
    Salt and pepper
2   teaspoons chopped fresh rosemary, or 1 teaspoon dried
4   thin slices provolone cheese, quartered
    Kitchen twine
4   thin rectangular slices boiled ham
1   teaspoon unsalted butter
1   teaspoon olive or other oil
½   cup water
    Lemon wedges, for serving

1. **ON A CUTTING BOARD,** cover the chicken breasts with plastic wrap and pound with a meat mallet or rolling pin to a little less than ½ inch thick. Sprinkle each with salt and pepper and ½ teaspoon rosemary. Cut each provolone slice in quarters and stack them. Place one stack of cheese on one half of each chicken breast, folding the other half over to cover.

2. **CUT EIGHT 10-INCH PIECES** of kitchen twine. Wrap a folded breast in a slice of ham and tie around the center with a piece of twine to secure. Give the breast a quarter turn, and tie again so that the two pieces of twine cross in the center. Tie up the remaining 3 breasts in the same way.

(continued)

3. IN A 10-INCH NONSTICK SKILLET, melt the butter with the oil over medium heat. Add the breasts and cook until nicely browned on one side, 3 to 4 minutes. Turn and brown on the other side, 3 to 4 minutes. Add the water to the pan, adjust the heat so it simmers, cover, and cook until the breasts are cooked through and the juices no longer run pink, 15 to 18 minutes. Cut off the twine with scissors and serve each stuffed breast with a lemon wedge.

Pork Tacos

It's taco time! Soft corn tortillas filled with chile-spiced lean pork and peppers for everyone's favorite fast food. Microwaving the tortillas keeps them warm and pliable and is a better choice than the usual fried tacos. The crunchy radish salad is a fresh take on an underused veggie.

SERVES 4

NUTRITION PER SERVING:
CALORIES 288, TOTAL FAT 6g, SODIUM 428mg, SUGARS 6g

8	red radishes, trimmed and quartered
1	tablespoon fresh lime juice
2	tablespoons chopped fresh cilantro
¾	teaspoon salt
1	¾-pound pork tenderloin, cut into ½-inch chunks
2	teaspoons chipotle chile powder
	Cooking spray
1	onion, diced
1	green bell pepper, stemmed, seeded, and diced
1	red bell pepper, stemmed, seeded, and diced
8	corn tortillas

1. **COMBINE THE RADISHES,** lime juice, cilantro, and ¼ teaspoon salt in a small bowl. Cover and refrigerate until ready to serve.

2. **COMBINE THE PORK,** chile powder, and ¼ teaspoon salt in a medium bowl and toss until the pork is evenly coated. Lightly coat a large skillet with cooking spray and set over medium-high heat. Add the pork and spread in a single layer. Cook, stirring occasionally, until browned and just cooked through, about 5 minutes. Using a slotted spoon, transfer to a large bowl.

(continued)

3. REMOVE THE SKILLET from the heat and lightly spray with cooking spray. Heat over medium-high heat and add the onion, peppers, and remaining 1/4 teaspoon salt and cook, stirring occasionally, until tender, about 8 minutes. Stir in the pork and its accumulated juices and cook 1 minute longer. Remove from the heat.

4. WRAP THE TORTILLAS in damp paper towels and microwave on High until warm and pliable, about 30 seconds. Divide the pork mixture among the tortillas and serve with the radish salad on the side.

NOTE: Try ancho or your favorite chile powder blend.

Asian Chicken Salad

You can lighten your usual chicken salad with light mayo—and you should. But try this Asian version the next time you get a craving. By adding flavorful and fragrant ingredients usually found in stir-fries, we've created a satisfying new twist on the familiar, and we've lowered the fat for you! These also make wonderful sandwiches with whole grain bread or pita pockets.

SERVES 4

NUTRITION PER SERVING:
CALORIES 246, TOTAL FAT 7g, SODIUM 429mg, SUGARS 3g

¼ cup light mayonnaise
1 teaspoon low-sodium soy sauce
½ teaspoon toasted sesame oil, divided
Zest and juice of 1 lime
½ red onion, finely chopped
2 tablespoons chopped cilantro (plus extra for garnish)
¼ teaspoon salt
Freshly ground pepper to taste
3 cups shredded roast chicken, skin discarded
8 ounces salad greens (baby arugula or spinach or mixed)
2 tomatoes, thinly sliced

1. **IN A LARGE BOWL,** add the mayonnaise, soy sauce, half the sesame oil, half the lime zest and juice, the onion, cilantro, salt, and pepper and mix well to combine. Add the chicken and toss to coat evenly.

2. **SPREAD THE SALAD GREENS** on a large platter or in individual bowls and top with 2 tomato slices. Sprinkle the remaining sesame oil and lime zest and juice over the greens and tomatoes. Evenly divide the chicken mixture over the greens and serve, garnished with extra cilantro if desired.

Flank Steak with Indian Salsa

Flank steak is a great choice when you have the urge for a steak. It cooks in an instant and is naturally low in fat. You can broil, pan sear, or grill it. This recipe replaces the usual steak seasonings with a curry blend. A shower of coconut and some crunchy cumin seeds create a vibrant salsa. Just be sure to look for unsweetened coconut flakes.

SERVES 4

NUTRITION PER SERVING:
CALORIES 257, TOTAL FAT 13g, SODIUM 567mg, SUGARS 2g

For the steak:
- 1 teaspoon canola oil
- 1 pound flank steak
- ½ teaspoon salt
- ⅛ teaspoon freshly ground pepper
- 1 tablespoon garam masala (or 1 tablespoon curry powder plus ½ teaspoon ground cinnamon)

For the salsa:
- 2 tablespoons cumin seeds (or 1 tablespoon ground cumin)
- ¼ cup unsweetened shredded coconut
- ½ pound green beans, blanched and chopped into 1-inch pieces
- 2 tablespoons chopped fresh cilantro
- 1 large tomato, diced
- 1 teaspoon salt
- ⅛ teaspoon freshly ground pepper
  Zest and juice of ½ lime

1. PREHEAT THE BROILER, stovetop grill pan, or grill to high heat.

2. SPREAD THE OIL evenly over the steak, season with salt and pepper, and massage the garam masala or curry powder mixture into the steak. Set aside.

3. HEAT A SMALL, DRY SKILLET over medium-high heat. Add the cumin seeds and toast, stirring frequently, until they are fragrant, about 30 seconds to 1 minute. Do not burn. (You don't need to toast the ground cumin if using.) Transfer to a medium bowl.

4. ADD ALL THE REMAINING INGREDIENTS for the salsa to the cumin seeds and set aside. The salsa can be made an hour in advance and kept refrigerated.

(continued)

5. **COOK THE STEAK** for 5 to 7 minutes per side for medium rare. Remove to a cutting board and let the meat rest for 5 minutes. Slice the steak thinly, in the opposite direction of the grain. Top with the salsa and serve immediately.

TIP: Letting the meat rest before slicing allows the juices to redistribute so they don't run out, which would happen if you immediately sliced the meat after cooking.

Orange Beef

Takeout food is tempting, but wait till you try our version of Chinese Orange Beef. We've cut out the frying but kept all the flavor. Chinese five-spice powder is usually available in the spice section of the grocery store. It's a combination of fragrant spices, but if you can't find it try substituting ⅛ teaspoon each ground cinnamon, ground cloves, ground ginger, and anise seeds or one whole star anise. Serve alongside a heaping bowl of steamed broccoli, string beans, or bok choy.

SERVES 4

NUTRITION PER SERVING:
CALORIES 229, TOTAL FAT 10g, SODIUM 218mg, SUGARS 4g

1   pound flank steak, cut into ⅛-inch-thick slices across the
    grain
2   teaspoons fresh ginger, grated
½   teaspoon five-spice powder
3   teaspoons low-sodium soy sauce
1   orange
3   tablespoons orange juice
2   teaspoons cornstarch
1   teaspoon canola oil
3   scallions, thinly sliced

1. COMBINE THE STEAK, ginger, five-spice powder, and 1 teaspoon soy sauce in a medium bowl. Marinate at room temperature while you prepare the other ingredients.

2. USING THE LARGE HOLES of a box grater, grate the zest of the orange into a small bowl. Peel the orange, then break it into segments and coarsely chop. In a small bowl, stir together the orange juice, cornstarch, and the remaining 2 teaspoons soy sauce.

(continued)

3. HEAT THE OIL in a nonstick 12-inch skillet over high heat. Add the steak and cook, undisturbed, for 1 minute. Continue cooking, stirring occasionally, until the meat just loses its pinkness. Add the scallions and reserved orange zest and cook, stirring, until fragrant, about 1 minute. Stir in the sauce mixture and cook, stirring occasionally, until the sauce bubbles and thickens, about 2 minutes. Garnish with the reserved orange segments and serve.

Chicken Meatballs

Baking the meatballs in the sauce cuts out the calories from the usual frying. Look for fire-roasted canned tomatoes; they add a terrific smokiness to the dish. Serve along with a slice of crusty bread and steamed spinach in place of the expected pasta.

SERVES 4

NUTRITION PER SERVING:
CALORIES 314, TOTAL FAT 13g, SODIUM 510mg, SUGARS 7g

	Cooking spray
1	pound ground chicken (use a mixture of dark and white meat)
1	cup fresh whole wheat bread crumbs
¼	cup skim milk
1	large egg, lightly beaten
1	small onion, finely chopped
¼	cup finely chopped fresh flat-leaf parsley leaves
2	tablespoons finely grated Parmesan cheese
¼	teaspoon salt
¼	teaspoon pepper
1	(14.5-ounce) can crushed tomatoes, preferably fire-roasted

1. **PREHEAT THE OVEN** to 450°F. Spray a large (11×13-inch) oven-safe baking dish with cooking spray.

2. **COMBINE THE CHICKEN,** bread crumbs, milk, egg, onion, parsley, Parmesan, salt, and pepper in a large bowl. Mix with your hands until well blended, then form into 12 meatballs. Arrange the meatballs in a single layer on the prepared pan.

3. **BAKE UNTIL BROWNED,** about 10 minutes. Carefully pour the tomatoes over and around the meatballs and bake until the meatballs are just cooked through and the tomatoes are hot, about 5 minutes longer. Serve immediately.

Pork with Apples

This rich and creamy dish is deeply satisfying and low in calories—and we've kept the cream. Lean loin pork chops cook up in a flash, and the touch of cream rounds out the tart sweetness of the apples. Comfort food without the calories, this will become a treasured family favorite.

SERVES 4

NUTRITION PER SERVING:
CALORIES 270, TOTAL FAT 9g, SODIUM 591mg, SUGARS 5g

1½ pounds loin pork chops, fat fully trimmed, off the bone
1   teaspoon salt
¼   teaspoon freshly ground pepper
    Cooking spray, preferably olive oil
1   shallot, peeled and finely chopped
1   apple, peeled, cored, and cut into eighths
¾   cup apple cider
2   tablespoons heavy cream

1. **LIGHTLY POUND** the pork with a meat mallet or rolling pin to flatten slightly.

2. **SEASON** with salt and pepper.

3. **LIGHTLY SPRAY** a large sauté pan with cooking spray and set over medium-high heat.

4. **ADD THE PORK** to the pan and cook 3 to 4 minutes. Turn and cook for another 4 minutes, until cooked through. Remove the pork to a plate and keep covered. Sauté the shallot and apple until slightly golden. Add the apple cider and cook until the liquid begins to boil. Add the heavy cream and stir. Return the pork to the pan, toss with the sauce, and serve immediately.

Cashew Chicken

This Chinese classic is usually brimming with cashews—and calories. The trick is using the cashews as a garnish to give you that satisfying crunch without extra calories. Try adding thinly sliced red peppers or string beans along with the broccoli.

SERVES 6

NUTRITION PER SERVING:
CALORIES 312, TOTAL FAT 15g, SODIUM 575mg, SUGARS 2g

¾ pound chicken tenders, halved
3 tablespoons low-sodium soy sauce
¾ cup low-sodium chicken broth
2 teaspoons cornstarch
½ teaspoon dark sesame oil
    Pinch of crushed red pepper
    Pinch of brown sugar
    Cooking spray
3 scallions, thinly sliced
3 garlic cloves, thinly sliced
1 (10-ounce) bag broccoli florets
2 cups cooked brown rice, for serving
¼ cup roasted cashew nuts, roughly chopped

1. **PLACE THE CHICKEN** in a small bowl, add 1 tablespoon soy sauce, and toss until thoroughly combined. Let sit for 5 minutes.

2. **IN A SMALL BOWL,** combine ¼ cup chicken broth, the remaining 2 tablespoons of soy sauce, the cornstarch, sesame oil, crushed red pepper, and brown sugar; set aside.

3. **SPRAY A LARGE NONSTICK SAUTÉ PAN** with cooking spray and place over high heat until hot. Add the chicken and quickly stir-fry until no longer pink, about 2 to 3 minutes. Transfer the chicken to a plate and cover loosely with aluminum foil to keep warm.

4. **ADD THE SCALLIONS** and garlic to the pan and cook until slightly softened and fragrant, about 30 seconds. Add the broccoli and remaining ½ cup of chicken broth and cook, stirring, until the broccoli is slightly tender but still crisp, about 2 to 3 minutes. Add the soy sauce mixture and return the chicken to the pan to reheat gently and thicken the sauce.

5. **TOSS TO COMBINE** thoroughly and serve immediately with rice, garnished with the chopped cashews.

Turkey Meatloaf with Dried Cranberries

The comforting flavors of Thanksgiving show up on one platter, with half the work! This meatloaf has a double cranberry boost—tucked inside the loaf and as a tart and tangy glaze on top. Parsnips bake alongside until they are caramelized and soft; their distinctive flavor is delicious. Try adding a few to the mix the next time you roast your usual potatoes and carrots.

SERVES 4

NUTRITION PER SERVING:
CALORIES 435, TOTAL FAT 16g, SODIUM 589mg, SUGARS 22g

½   cup dried cranberries
1   slice whole wheat bread
⅓   cup skim milk
1   pound ground turkey
1   small onion, finely chopped
1   carrot, peeled and finely chopped
½   cup chopped fresh flat-leaf parsley
1   large egg white
½   teaspoon salt
½   teaspoon pepper
2   tablespoons olive oil
2   tablespoons Dijon mustard
1   pound parsnips, trimmed, peeled, cored,
     and cut into 2-inch lengths

1. **PREHEAT THE OVEN** to 400°F. Line a 13×9-inch baking pan with aluminum foil.

2. **PLACE 1/4 CUP** of cranberries in a small heatproof bowl. Pour boiling water over to cover and let soak until softened, about 10 minutes.

3. **GRIND THE BREAD** in a food processor to fine crumbs and transfer to a large bowl. Pour the milk over the crumbs and let soften for 1 minute. Add the turkey, onion, carrot, parsley, egg white, salt, pepper,

1 tablespoon oil, and the remaining ¼ cup cranberries. Mix with your hands until everything is well combined.

4. **TRANSFER THE MIXTURE** to the prepared pan and shape into a 9×5-inch loaf. Drain the softened cranberries and place in the food processor along with the mustard. Process until smooth, then spread over the meatloaf.

5. **TOSS THE PARSNIPS** with the remaining tablespoon of oil. Scatter around the meatloaf in the pan.

6. **BAKE UNTIL THE MEATLOAF** is cooked through (a thermometer inserted in the center should register 170°F) and the parsnips are browned, about 1 hour.

Better-for-You Meat Sauce with Pasta

This sauce is better for you because half the usual beef is replaced with an eggplant, which also adds a deeper, richer flavor. The eggplant melts down so picky eaters won't even know it's there! For a totally veggie version use twice the amount of eggplant and add 2 cubed zucchini. This freezes really well too, and can be easily doubled; just use two pans or cook in batches.

SERVES 6

NUTRITION PER SERVING, SAUCE:
CALORIES 181, TOTAL FAT 8g, SODIUM 896mg, SUGARS 12g

NUTRITION PER SERVING, PASTA:
CALORIES 47, TOTAL FAT less than 1g, SODIUM 1mg, SUGARS less than 1g

1	tablespoon olive oil
½	pound 85% lean ground beef
1	teaspoon salt
¼	teaspoon freshly ground pepper
½	yellow onion, finely chopped
2	garlic cloves, peeled and chopped
2	carrots, chopped
1	eggplant, peeled and cut into small cubes
¼	teaspoon dried thyme, or 3 sprigs fresh
¼	teaspoon dried oregano, or 3 sprigs fresh
	Pinch of cayenne
4	cups tomato sauce
	Pinch of sugar
½	pound whole wheat penne or spaghetti, cooked

1. HEAT THE OIL in a large Dutch oven over medium-high heat. Add the beef and cook, stirring frequently, until the meat is golden brown. Season with half the salt and pepper. Remove the meat to a small bowl with a slotted spoon, set aside, and discard all but 1 tablespoon of fat from the pan.

2. **LOWER THE HEAT** slightly, add the onion, the garlic, the carrots, and eggplant, and cook, stirring frequently, until the vegetables are golden. If they are sticking to the pan, add a few tablespoons of water. Season with the remaining salt and pepper, herbs, and cayenne. Stir in the tomato sauce and sugar.

3. **CAREFULLY DRAIN** any fat from the meat. Return the meat to the pot. Stir, bring to a boil, cover, and lower the heat so the sauce simmers. Simmer for 30 minutes and remove the cover for the last 5 minutes of cooking time.

4. **TASTE AND ADJUST** the seasoning if necessary. Remove the fresh herbs if used. Serve over pasta.

Oven-Fried Chicken with Cinnamon Spice

No need to give up fried chicken—wait till you try our version, with a fragrant spice blend. The cinnamon is the secret ingredient you just can't seem to place; it adds a new dimension to the crust. Dried bread crumbs provide the crunch; try whole wheat if you can find them.

SERVES 4

NUTRITION PER SERVING:
CALORIES 407, TOTAL FAT 8g, SODIUM 590mg, SUGARS 3g

1	cup whole wheat or plain dried bread crumbs
1	teaspoon onion powder
1	teaspoon garlic powder
½	teaspoon ground cinnamon
½	teaspoon salt
½	teaspoon freshly ground pepper
1	tablespoon canola oil
½	cup all-purpose flour
1	large egg, lightly beaten
4	boneless, skinless chicken breasts (about 1½ pounds)

1. **PREHEAT THE OVEN** to 450°F. Line a large rimmed baking sheet with aluminum foil.

2. **COMBINE THE BREAD CRUMBS,** onion powder, garlic powder, cinnamon, ¼ teaspoon salt, ¼ teaspoon pepper, and the canola oil in a shallow dish. Place the flour in another shallow dish. Place the egg in another shallow dish.

3. **SEASON THE CHICKEN** with the remaining ¼ teaspoon salt and ¼ teaspoon pepper. Coat a chicken breast in the flour, shaking off the excess. Then dip in the egg and dredge in the crumb mixture. Place the chicken in the prepared pan. Repeat with the remaining chicken breast halves.

4. **BAKE UNTIL THE CHICKEN** is golden and cooked through, about 15 minutes.

Coconut Chicken and Tropical Salsa

Feel the ocean breeze yet? This dish perks up the table during the dark winter and is great for parties any time of the year. Cornflakes and coconut team up to provide the crispy crust. You'll find yourself spooning this salsa over grilled meat and fish too! Add some cayenne or pass the hot sauce if you want to turn up the heat even more, and serve with a pitcher of our Pineapple Mojitos (page 61).

SERVES 4

NUTRITION PER SERVING:
CALORIES 479, TOTAL FAT 24g, SODIUM 876mg, SUGARS 8g

1	large egg
2	cups cornflakes, coarsely crushed
½	cup shredded unsweetened coconut
1	pound chicken tenders
½	teaspoon salt
½	teaspoon pepper
1	cup diced fresh pineapple
1	cup corn kernels, thawed if frozen
1	red bell pepper, stemmed, seeded, and diced
1	scallion, thinly sliced
2	teaspoons fresh lime juice
1	teaspoon canola oil

1. **PREHEAT THE OVEN** to 425°F. Line a large rimmed baking sheet with aluminum foil.

2. **CRACK THE EGG** into a shallow dish and beat lightly. Combine the cornflakes and coconut in another shallow dish. Season the chicken with ¼ teaspoon salt and ¼ teaspoon pepper, then dip in the egg and dredge in the cornflake mixture.

(continued)

3. ARRANGE THE COATED CHICKEN on the prepared pan in a single layer. Bake until golden brown and cooked through, about 10 to 12 minutes.

4. MEANWHILE, toss together the pineapple, corn, pepper, scallion, lime juice, oil, remaining ¼ teaspoon salt, and remaining ¼ teaspoon pepper in a large bowl.

5. SERVE THE CHICKEN with the salsa.

Fettuccine con Funghi

Creamy fettuccine, earthy mushrooms, half the calories—what's the secret? Evaporated nonfat milk, freshly grated Parmesan, and fresh herbs! Look for the most interesting variety of mushrooms the market offers for bigger flavor.

SERVES 4

NUTRITION PER SERVING:
CALORIES 251, TOTAL FAT 10g, SODIUM 843mg, SUGARS 6g

1½ teaspoons salt
2   teaspoons olive oil
3   garlic cloves, peeled and smashed
1   pound mushrooms, thinly sliced (any combination of shiitake, cremini, portabello, and white)
¼   cup heavy cream
6   tablespoons nonfat evaporated milk
12   ounces whole wheat fettuccine
¼   cup grated Parmesan cheese
1   tablespoon fresh rosemary, chopped, or 1½ teaspoons dried
1   tablespoon chopped fresh parsley
⅛   teaspoon freshly ground black pepper

1. BRING A LARGE POT of water and half of the salt to a boil.

2. IN A LARGE SAUTÉ PAN, heat the oil with the garlic over medium heat until the garlic turns lightly golden brown, about 1 minute. Add the mushrooms and the remaining salt and sauté, stirring occasionally, until the mushrooms are golden brown, about 3 minutes. Stir in the cream and evaporated milk, bring to a boil, and simmer for 1 minute.

3. MEANWHILE, add the fettuccine to the boiling water and cook until al dente, about 8 minutes. Drain, reserving about ½ cup of the pasta cooking water. Add the drained fettuccine to the saucepan with the mushrooms and add a little of the reserved pasta cooking water if the mixture is dry. Stir in the Parmesan along with the herbs and black pepper.

4. DIVIDE THE PASTA among 4 warm serving bowls.

Pasta with Sausage and Cherry Tomatoes

Yes, you can keep your sausage and pasta! And if you always keep sausages on hand in your freezer, this is an instant supper that's satisfying and simple. Try substituting turkey sausage along with feta and spinach and adding oregano instead of the thyme for a Greek twist, and garnish with lemon wedges.

SERVES 4

NUTRITION PER SERVING:
CALORIES 283, TOTAL FAT 19g, SODIUM 420mg, SUGARS 2g

	Olive oil cooking spray
½	pound pork sausages, removed from their casings and crumbled
2	garlic cloves, finely chopped
	Pinch of hot pepper flakes
16	cherry tomatoes
1	teaspoon chopped fresh thyme
	Salt and pepper
7	ounces whole wheat linguine, cooked al dente
1	teaspoon extra virgin olive oil
1	tablespoon chopped fresh parsley

1. SPRAY A LARGE NONSTICK SKILLET with olive oil cooking spray and place over medium-high heat. Add the sausage and stir occasionally for about 3 minutes, until the meat begins to brown. Add the garlic, pepper flakes, tomatoes, and thyme. Cook until the sausage turns dark brown and the tomato skins have burst, about another 3 to 4 minutes. Season with salt and pepper.

2. PLACE THE COOKED PASTA in a warm serving bowl and toss with extra virgin olive oil. Top the pasta with the sausage and tomato mixture, stir to combine, and sprinkle with parsley.

Mussels

If you love mussels, you'll love this dish. If you've never made them or tried them, this is the recipe to start with—it's super quick, impressive, and delicious!

Simply sauté some aromatic fennel (or onion if you don't love fennel's signature licorce flavor), toss in the mussels, finish with herbs, *et voilà*! You'll be transported to the French seaside in no time. And farmed mussels come very well cleaned and are a more affordable shellfish.

SERVES 4 AS A MAIN COURSE, 6 AS A STARTER

NUTRITION PER SERVING:
CALORIES 402, TOTAL FAT 11g, SODIUM 1121mg, SUGARS 2g

2   pounds live mussels in shells
2   teaspoons extra virgin olive oil
2   garlic cloves, peeled and slightly smashed
½   fennel bulb, thinly sliced (or ½ sweet onion, thinly sliced)
1   cup white wine
1   cup water
½   teaspoon salt, divided
1   tablespoon finely chopped fresh tarragon
1   tablespoon finely chopped fresh parsley
2   tablespoons heavy cream
⅛   teaspoon freshly ground pepper
4   thin slices crusty bread
     Fresh lemon, quartered, for garnish

1. **RINSE THE MUSSELS** and pull off any "beard"—the stringy bits. Discard any mussels that are opened, as these are unsafe to eat.

2. **IN A LARGE,** heavy pot over medium heat, add the oil, garlic, and fennel and sauté until the fennel is translucent, about 5 to 7 minutes. Add the wine and water, and add ¼ teaspoon salt and the herbs, and bring to a boil. Add the mussels, cover, and cook for 5 to 6 minutes,

stirring the mussels midway through to ensure even cooking. The mussels should now all be opened. If not, cook for an additional 1 to 2 minutes. Pour in the heavy cream and pepper. Toss, and taste the broth, adding the additional salt if needed.

3. DIVIDE THE MUSSELS and broth among 4 warm bowls and serve with a slice of crusty bread for dipping. Garnish with lemon.

Shrimp and Grits

If you don't know this beloved Southern classic, here's a new comfort food for your repertoire. A medley of salty, creamy, sweet, and a kick of heat—it's super fast to prepare and perfect for a busy weeknight supper. Instant grits are usually found in the breakfast aisle and are a clever swap for pasta too.

SERVES 4

NUTRITION PER SERVING:
CALORIES 242, TOTAL FAT 6g, SODIUM 853mg, SUGARS 5g

¾	cup quick 5-minute grits
1	cup skim milk
1	cup water
¾	teaspoon salt
2	tablespoons freshly grated Parmesan cheese
3	teaspoons olive oil
1	pint grape or cherry tomatoes
¼	teaspoon pepper
12	ounces medium shrimp, peeled and deveined
1-2	teaspoons hot sauce, or to your taste
	Chopped fresh parsley, for garnish

1. **COMBINE THE GRITS,** milk, water, and ½ teaspoon salt in a large saucepan. Bring to a boil, then reduce the heat to low and simmer, covered, stirring occasionally, until the grits are creamy and soft, about 5 to 6 minutes. Stir in the Parmesan, remove from heat, and keep warm.

2. **HEAT THE OIL** in a large sauté pan over medium-high heat. Add the tomatoes, the remaining ¼ teaspoon of salt, the pepper, and the shrimp, and sauté for 3 to 5 minutes, until the tomatoes have collapsed and the shrimp are opaque and fully cooked. Add hot sauce to taste.

3. **SPOON THE SHRIMP** and tomatoes over the grits, sprinkle with parsley if desired, and serve.

Cod Saltimbocca

A twist on the expected veal, this dish will sway even confirmed fish haters! Wrapped in crispy prosciutto, the mild cod is served on a bed of creamy beans peppered with radicchio slivers. It's restaurant sophistication without a lot of fuss—all in a flash!

SERVES 4

NUTRITION PER SERVING:
CALORIES 242, TOTAL FAT 3g, SODIUM 562mg, SUGARS 2g

4	(6-ounce) cod fillets, bones removed
¼	teaspoon freshly ground pepper
4	fresh sage leaves
4	thin slices lean prosciutto
1	teaspoon extra virgin olive oil
2	garlic cloves, finely chopped
1	(12-ounce) can white cannellini beans, rinsed well and drained
	Freshly ground pepper
½	small head of radicchio, cut into ribbons like cabbage
1	teaspoon balsamic vinegar
	Extra virgin olive oil spray

1. **RINSE THE COD FILLETS** and pat dry. Sprinkle each fillet with pepper and top with a sage leaf. Wrap the prosciutto around the fish and set aside.

2. **IN A SMALL SAUCEPAN,** add the olive oil and place over medium heat. Add the garlic, beans, and freshly ground pepper. Add the radicchio and balsamic vinegar, toss to combine, and check the seasoning. Keep warm while cooking the fish.

3. **SPRAY A LARGE** nonstick sauté pan with the olive oil spray and place over medium-high heat. Add the cod and cook for about 5 minutes per side, until the prosciutto is crisp and the interior of the fish is opaque.

4. **SPOON THE BEAN MIXTURE** onto the plate and top with the cod. Serve immediately.

BBQ Salmon

This sauce is our secret weapon. We brush it on chicken breasts or wings, steaks, and even veggies before grilling or even broiling. Yes, we confess, it's delish on ribs too, but it's hard for us to stop at one rib, so we've switched to fish. It's perfect with this salmon, especially when served with our Southwestern Slaw (page 130).

The maple provides a rich sweetness, cumin delivers the signature BBQ spice, and you'll love the slight kick from the mustard and chile. The soy brings it all together. Make a double batch and keep the rest in the fridge for a few days.

SERVES 4

NUTRITION PER SERVING:
CALORIES 402, TOTAL FAT 23g, SODIUM 667mg, SUGARS 10g

- ¼ cup ketchup
- 2   tablespoons pure maple syrup
- 2   tablespoons low-sodium soy sauce
- 1   tablespoon mustard
- ¼ teaspoon ancho chile powder
- ¼ teaspoon ground cumin
- 1   garlic clove, peeled and smashed
- 4   (6-ounce) salmon fillets or steaks, skin removed if using fillet

1. **PREHEAT A MEDIUM-HOT GRILL** or preheat the oven to 400°F.

2. **IF USING THE OVEN,** line a baking sheet with aluminum foil.

3. **IN A SMALL SAUCEPAN,** combine all the ingredients except the salmon and cook over medium-low heat for 5 minutes. Set aside to cool slightly (this can be done a few days ahead and refrigerated).

4. **BRUSH THE TOP** of the salmon with the BBQ sauce and place on the grill or in the oven and cook until the desired doneness, about 5 minutes for medium rare or 7 to 10 minutes for medium. Turn the fish midway through cooking.

Shrimp Scampi

At most restaurants, you'll find this shrimp swimming in fattening butter. Here we've replaced the butter with a slurry of cornstarch and water and added a drizzle of olive oil to provide the signature Italian flavor. We've put back just enough of the butter, tossed with an earthy whole wheat pasta so you won't feel deprived.

SERVES 4

NUTRITION PER SERVING:
CALORIES 427, TOTAL FAT 11g, SODIUM 567mg, SUGARS 3g

8	ounces whole wheat or regular linguine
1½	teaspoons cornstarch
1½	teaspoons cold water
1½	tablespoons olive oil
2	garlic cloves, sliced
1	pound medium to large shrimp, shelled
½	teaspoon salt
¼	teaspoon red pepper flakes
¼	cup dry white wine
½	cup low-sodium, reduced-fat chicken stock
3	scallions (white and green parts), sliced
3	tablespoons chopped fresh parsley
2	tablespoons chopped (or torn) fresh basil
1	teaspoon unsalted butter
⅓	cup finely grated Parmesan cheese (optional)
	Freshly ground black pepper

1. **BRING A LARGE POT** of water to a boil for the pasta. Add the pasta and cook according to package directions.

2. **MEANWHILE, IN A SMALL BOWL,** stir together the cornstarch and cold water; set aside.

(continued)

3. **HEAT THE OLIVE OIL** with the garlic in a large nonstick pan over medium heat until the garlic is fragrant but not brown. Sprinkle the shrimp with salt. Add to the pan and cook, turning, until the shrimp turns pink on both sides, 1½ to 2 minutes. Stir in the red pepper flakes. Add the wine and simmer 1 minute. Remove the shrimp to a plate and keep covered. Add the chicken stock to the pan and bring to a simmer. Stir in the cornstarch mixture and return to a boil. Remove from the heat. Add the scallions and herbs.

4. **WHEN THE PASTA IS COOKED,** drain in a colander. Return the shrimp to the skillet, add the butter, and cook over medium heat, tossing in the sauce, until warm, 1 to 2 minutes. Transfer the pasta to the serving bowl, add the contents of the skillet, and toss. Sprinkle with cheese, if desired, and pepper and serve.

Swordfish Arrabiata

While *arrabiata* may mean "angry" in Italian (the name coming from the heat of the pepper flakes), you'll be nothing but happy with this flavorful pasta dish. It's fancy enough to impress your friends, and fast enough for a family supper.

SERVES 4

NUTRITION PER SERVING:

CALORIES 319, TOTAL FAT 12g, SODIUM 765mg, SUGARS 8g

1	pound swordfish (about 2 large steaks), cut into 1-inch cubes
1	teaspoon salt
	Freshly ground black pepper
2	tablespoons extra virgin olive oil
1	onion, chopped
3	garlic cloves, peeled
½	teaspoon crushed red pepper flakes
2	cups chopped canned Italian plum tomatoes
2	teaspoons finely chopped fresh rosemary
½	pound whole wheat fettuccine, cooked, for serving

1. **SEASON THE FISH** with half the salt and some pepper. Heat the oil in a large sauté pan over medium-high heat. Add the fish and cook, stirring occasionally, until the fish is opaque, about 1 minute. Transfer the fish to a small bowl and set aside.

2. **LOWER THE HEAT** and add the onion and garlic to the pan along with the remaining salt and the crushed red pepper flakes. Cook until the onion is lightly golden, about 3 minutes. Add the tomatoes and bring the mixture to a boil. Add the rosemary, lower the heat, and simmer for 5 minutes.

3. **RETURN THE FISH** and any juices to the pan and gently stir to reheat the fish, about 1 minute.

4. **SERVE OVER PASTA** and sprinkle with a bit of salt.

Fish Kebabs with Roasted Red Pepper Sauce

Kebabs are a smart way to make sure you are getting enough veggies, and they're stylish and delicious when served with our roasted red pepper sauce. You can swap the swordfish for chunks of cod or salmon, and try adding mushrooms or even fennel or onion chunks along with the zucchini.

SERVES 4, TWO SKEWERS PER PERSON

NUTRITION PER SERVING:
CALORIES 320, TOTAL FAT 15g, SODIUM 728mg, SUGARS 5g

NUTRITION PER SERVING, SAUCE:
CALORIES 50, TOTAL FAT 2g, SODIUM 323mg, SUGARS 4g

8	skewers (if using wood or bamboo, soak for 30 minutes beforehand)
1	pound swordfish, cut into ½-inch chunks
2	zucchini, cut into ½-inch chunks
2	yellow squash, cut into ½-inch chunks
3	thick slices crusty bread, cut into 8 ½-inch chunks
8	cherry tomatoes

Marinade:

3	tablespoons extra virgin olive oil
1	tablespoon red wine vinegar
2	tablespoons fresh herbs (basil, parsley, or rosemary), chopped, or 1 tablespoon dried
½	teaspoon paprika
1	teaspoon salt
¼	teaspoon freshly ground pepper

1. **LINE A BAKING SHEET** with aluminum foil and set aside.

2. **SKEWER ONE PIECE** of fish, one zucchini chunk, and one yellow squash chunk. Repeat, continuing almost to the end, then top with one chunk of bread and one cherry tomato. Repeat with the remaining skewers, for a total of 8 skewers. Place on foil-lined tray and set aside.

3. **TO MAKE THE MARINADE,** in a small bowl mix the olive oil, vinegar, herbs, paprika, salt, and pepper. Using a pastry brush, brush the kebabs

with the marinade. This can be done up to 3 hours in advance if the kebabs are stored in the refrigerator.

4. **PREPARE A HOT GRILL,** or set the oven broiler to High. Grill or broil the skewers, for about 2 to 3 minutes per side, until the fish is cooked through. Serve with Roasted Red Pepper Sauce.

Roasted Red Pepper Sauce

½   cup reduced fat mayonnaise
2   roasted and peeled red peppers, finely chopped
1   teaspoon lemon juice
⅛   teaspoon salt
     Freshly ground pepper, to taste

IN A MEDIUM BOWL, combine and mix all the ingredients together. Transfer to a serving bowl and serve alongside kebabs.

Fish and Chips

Give up fish and chips? Never. Okay, so you do have to give up the fried version, and using cornflakes for the crunch is a clever swap. You can use any potatoes you have on hand, but these golden Yukons have a slight sweetness and wonderful texture. Use coarse salt for extra crunch. If you have a bit of room in your calorie count, serve with a few table-spoons of light mayo that's been mixed with a generous pinch of Old Bay seasoning and fresh lemon for dipping.

SERVES 4

NUTRITION PER SERVING:
CALORIES 359, TOTAL FAT 12g, SODIUM 347mg, SUGARS 1g

4	Yukon gold potatoes, scrubbed
3	tablespoons olive oil
1/2	teaspoon salt, preferably coarse sea salt
1/4	teaspoon pepper
1 1/2	cups cornflakes, crushed
2	large egg whites
1/4	cup all-purpose flour
1 1/2	pounds white fish fillets, cut into 5×1-inch strips
1/4	teaspoon cayenne

1. **CENTER ONE OVEN RACK** in the oven and arrange a second rack in the position closest to the broiler. Preheat the oven to 450°F. Line 2 large rimmed baking sheets with nonstick aluminum foil.

2. **CUT EACH POTATO** lengthwise into 1/4-inch slices, then cut each slice lengthwise into 1/4-inch-thick pieces to form "fries." Toss with 2 table-spoons of oil, 1/4 teaspoon of salt, and the pepper. Spread in a single layer on one prepared baking sheet. Bake on the middle rack until golden brown and crisp, carefully stirring occasionally, about 25 minutes.

(continued)

3. MEANWHILE, combine the crushed cornflakes and remaining 1 table-spoon of oil in a shallow dish. In another shallow dish, beat the egg whites until foamy. Spread the flour in a thin layer in a third shallow dish. Season the fish with the remaining 1/4 teaspoon of salt and the cayenne. Coat the fish with flour, shaking off any excess. Dip into the egg whites, then dredge in the crumb mixture, patting on the crumbs to cover. Arrange the fish in a single layer on the remaining prepared pan. Bake on the rack closest to the broiler until cooked through, about 6 to 8 minutes, turning midway through baking.

4. REMOVE THE POTATOES from the oven and reset the oven control to Broil. For extra crunch, broil the fish until the crumbs are golden brown, about 2 minutes. Serve with the potatoes.

Quick Jambalaya

This is our riff on a jamming jambalaya that takes half the time and leaves out most of the fat and calories. A store-bought turkey drumstick cuts out the usual frying time and provides the deep smoky flavor of the usual roux.

SERVES 4

NUTRITION PER SERVING:
CALORIES 349, TOTAL FAT 8g, SODIUM 890mg, SUGARS 8g

1	smoked turkey drumstick (about ½ pound)
2	teaspoons vegetable oil
1	small onion, chopped
1	small green bell pepper, chopped
1	celery stalk, chopped
1	(15-ounce) can diced tomatoes, drained
1½	cups water
¼	teaspoon salt
½	teaspoon Cajun spice
1	cup long-grain white rice

1. **CUT THE TURKEY MEAT** off the bone, then pull off and discard the tendons and skin from the meat. Cut the turkey into ½-inch pieces.

2. **HEAT THE OIL** in a 4-quart saucepan over medium-high heat, then cook the onion, bell pepper, and celery, stirring frequently, until the onion begins to brown, about 5 minutes.

3. **ADD THE TURKEY,** tomatoes, water, salt, and Cajun spice and bring to a boil, covered, over high heat. Stir in the rice and bring to a full rolling boil. Cover, reduce the heat to low, and cook until the rice is tender and the liquid is absorbed, about 20 minutes. Remove from the heat and let stand, covered, for 5 minutes. Fluff with a fork and serve, along with extra hot sauce.

Spaghetti Surprise

This is a dish that surprises kids of all ages—watching the "spaghetti" magically appear as the fork creates the strands. Spaghetti squash is great to keep on hand during the fall and winter months and it's versatile—try stirring in a bit of pesto, or sprinkle with cinnamon and a bit of dried sage to serve along with roast turkey breast.

SERVES 4

NUTRITION PER SERVING:
CALORIES 306, TOTAL FAT 13g, SODIUM 777mg, SUGARS 11g

1   large spaghetti squash
2   tablespoons extra virgin olive oil
    Salt and freshly ground pepper
1   garlic clove, peeled and finely chopped
2   cups prepared marinara sauce
2   tablespoons grated Parmesan cheese

1. PREHEAT THE OVEN to 400°F.

2. CUT THE SQUASH in half lengthwise and scoop and discard all seeds. Rub the squash inside and out with 1 tablespoon of oil and season the inside with salt and pepper. Place the squash, cut side down, on a baking sheet and cover with aluminum foil. Place in the oven and cook for 45 minutes, or until the rind is slightly soft and gives with a little pressure.

3. WITH A FORK, scrape the flesh out into an ovenproof bowl, creating the thin strands of "spaghetti." Cover and keep warm in a very low oven. This can be done ahead and rewarmed in a low oven or microwave.

4. MEANWHILE, heat a large sauté pan over medium heat and add the remaining tablespoon of oil and the garlic. Stir until the garlic is lightly golden, about 30 seconds, then add the marinara sauce and simmer until warm.

5. PLACE THE SQUASH STRANDS in 4 pasta bowls, top with the sauce, and sprinkle with the cheese. Serve immediately.

Helen

BEFORE: Size 8   **AFTER:** Size 6; lost 6 pounds

Helen really had her hands full. As a busy mom/author she was tackling many challenges all at once. Since she worked at home she often left her desk to raid the fridge—plus she had to juggle all the different family meals while trying to teach her sons healthy eating habits. She carried all that around as well as an extra ten pounds! CYT *really saved the day for Helen.*

"I have been a serial dieter for as long as I can remember, always looking for the next magic pill to lose weight. After having two boys I was walking around with an unwanted ten pounds—those last ten pounds that feel impossible to lose—and was skeptical about *CYT*'s approach because there were no gimmicks. I had a hard time believing you could lose weight without starving, without cutting out entire food groups, and without feeling deprived of favorites. BUT I was pleasantly surprised!!

"*CYT*'s approach, first and foremost, seemed to be: Food is our friend. It is not something to be scared of, intimidated by, or avoided. Cooking can be adventurous, flavorful, and fun—and you can still lose weight. I took this opportunity as a chance to spend more time in the kitchen playing with food! And I invited my children to play with me. We all loved trying new recipes and because the base ingredients were so manageable, I felt brave enough to edit and add as seemed fit. I mean, swapping sweet potatoes for russets, adding cauliflower to cupcakes (I kid you not!), and doubling the recipes to have satisfying meals on hand always helped me finally make peace with food. Plus, since the ingredients were easy to find, seasonal, and easily inter-changeable, our grocery bill was less too! It was so freeing not to be locked into stiff recipes with exotic ingredients that have to be followed to the letter. As a working mother, I found these recipes were user friendly, so I stuck with it!

"For the first time my whole family was able to eat the same foods instead of being subjected to Mom's wacky diet foods or having to make a different meal for everyone in the family. But most of all, I learned to love my kitchen; cooking is no longer a chore or a threat. Planning menus, preparing meals, and (YIKES!) enjoying what I am eating has made it possible for me to lose weight and I continue to lose. My husband and I look and feel great, the kids are learning to make healthier choices, and we are all coming to the table with smiles, leaving satisfied, and finding new ways to enjoy our food and our family!

"Thank you, *CYT*!!"

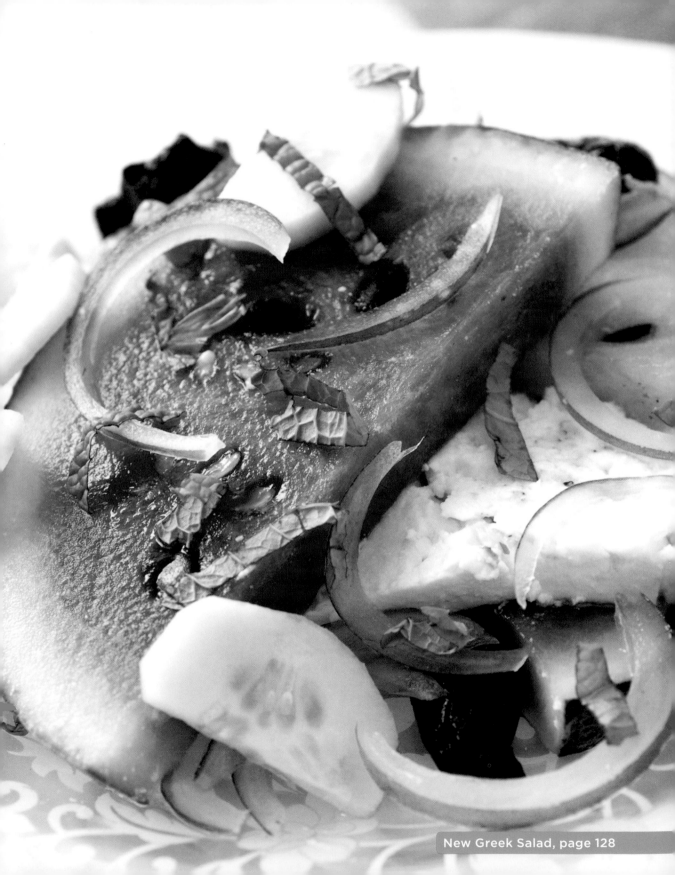

New Greek Salad, page 128

Sides/Soups/ Salads

Wondering what to serve alongside a main dish, or looking for a light supper or quick lunch idea?

Fresh, flavorful, and fast—here are some familiar and unexpected ideas with big flavors and small calorie counts!

Red, White, and Blue Potato Salad

Don't let the patriotic title stop you from making this any day of the week. The blue cheese dressing has all the richness you crave from a creamy potato salad with less than half the calories and fat. Be sure to sprinkle the potatoes with the vinegar and salt while still warm; this intensifies the flavor.

SERVES 4

NUTRITION PER SERVING:
CALORIES 150, TOTAL FAT 4g, SODIUM 334mg, SUGARS 3g

½   teaspoon salt, divided
1¼   pounds new potatoes, halved
1   teaspoon cider vinegar
⅓   cup reduced-fat sour cream
1   teaspoon water
2   tablespoons crumbled blue cheese
2   tablespoons chopped scallions
     Freshly ground pepper

1. FILL A LARGE SAUCEPAN with cold water, ¼ teaspoon of salt, and the potatoes and place over high heat. Bring the water to a boil and let the potatoes simmer for about 10 to 14 minutes, or until tender when pierced with the tip of a knife.

2. DRAIN THE POTATOES in a colander and transfer to a large bowl. Sprinkle with the remaining salt and vinegar and toss. Add the sour cream, water, blue cheese, and scallions. Taste and season with pepper and additional salt if desired.

Carrot Soup with a Kick

Carrot soup may seem familiar and not that inspiring—until you try this version, which is a far cry from bland or boring. This is a great anytime recipe—you probably already have carrots on hand, and curry powder is an easy way to add a kick to your basic favorites. The yogurt garnish can be swirled into the soup with a knife before serving.

SERVES 4

NUTRITION PER SERVING:
CALORIES 238, TOTAL FAT 6g, SODIUM 752mg, SUGARS 18g

1	tablespoon extra virgin olive oil
1	small onion, chopped
2	garlic cloves, chopped
2	teaspoons curry powder
1	teaspoon salt
⅛	teaspoon freshly ground pepper
	Zest and juice of 1 orange
5	cups vegetable or low-sodium chicken stock
2	pounds carrots, peeled and chopped
1	cup nonfat Greek-style yogurt
2	tablespoons chopped fresh cilantro

1. HEAT THE OLIVE OIL in a large pot over medium heat. Add the onion and garlic and cook until softened. Add the curry powder, salt, and pepper and stir constantly for 20 seconds, taking care not to burn the spices. Add the orange juice and cook for about 1 minute. Add the stock and carrots and bring the soup to a boil. Lower the heat and simmer until the carrots are soft and fully cooked, about 20 to 30 minutes.

2. MEANWHILE, in a small bowl, combine the orange zest, yogurt, and cilantro. Season to taste with salt and pepper and set aside.

(continued)

3. BLEND THE SOUP using a food processor, blender, or hand blender. (If using a processor or blender, do not overfill, and blend in batches if necessary.)

4. TOP WITH A DOLLOP of the yogurt mixture for garnish. Or place in the center of the soup bowl and using the tip of a knife, pull the knife through the yogurt to make a pretty pattern.

Hearty Vegetable and Lentil Soup

This soup is super versatile—you can swap the veggies for any of your favorites. Lentils are a healthy way to feel full and get your protein fix, and the ginger rounds out the flavors in a surprising way. For a smoother version puree the soup in batches in a blender or food processor.

SERVES 4

NUTRITION PER SERVING:
CALORIES 230, TOTAL FAT 4g, SODIUM 571mg, SUGARS 5g

1 tablespoon extra virgin olive oil
1 onion, thinly sliced
3 garlic cloves, peeled and crushed
1-inch piece of fresh ginger, peeled and grated
    or finely chopped
2 carrots, peeled and chopped
2 potatoes, peeled and cut into small cubes
½ pound lentils
1½ quarts water
1 vegetable stock cube
2 tablespoons Worcestershire sauce
2 teaspoons sherry vinegar
¼ teaspoon salt (optional)
    Freshly ground pepper
    Few dashes of hot sauce to taste

1. IN A LARGE SAUCEPAN or Dutch oven, heat the olive oil over medium-high heat and sauté the onion, garlic, and ginger, stirring frequently, for about 3 to 5 minutes, until softened but not colored. Add the carrots, potatoes, lentils, and water. Bring the soup to a boil, lower the heat, and simmer for 30 minutes.

2. ADD THE STOCK CUBE, Worcestershire, and sherry vinegar. Taste and add the salt if needed. Add the pepper and hot sauce. Serve immediately.

Cheese "Fries"

Okay, so these aren't exactly the cheese fries from the late-night bar menu. But they are a rustic treat and so much better for you! Butternut squash is a versatile veggie, and it's often readily available presliced in the produce aisle. Try this with your favorite root vegetable.

SERVES 4

NUTRITION PER SERVING:
CALORIES 103, TOTAL FAT 5g, SODIUM 563mg, SUGARS 3g

1   large butternut squash, peeled and seeded
1   tablespoon olive oil
1   teaspoon salt
¼   teaspoon pepper
¼   cup grated Parmesan cheese

1. PREHEAT THE OVEN to 450°F and line a sheet pan with aluminum foil.

2. CUT SQUASH into ¼-inch "french fries."

3. TOSS THE SQUASH with the olive oil and spread on the pan. Season with the salt and pepper.

4. BAKE FOR 30 MINUTES, shaking the pan until the squash "fries" are roasted and golden, tossing and turning the fries midway through baking.

5. SPRINKLE WITH THE PARMESAN and return to the oven for 2 minutes, until the cheese is melted.

New Greek Salad

We adore the classic Greek salad, with briny olives, slightly sharp feta cheese, and the best tomatoes, cukes, and greens. But we also love this modern version made with watermelon that's popping up in the hottest restaurants! It also looks gorgeous when arranged on a flat white platter in the center of the table along with our Blush Sangria (page 50) at brunch.

SERVES 4

NUTRITION PER SERVING:
CALORIES 291, TOTAL FAT 22g, SODIUM 540mg, SUGARS 7g

2	cups watermelon, seeded and cut into chunks or thin triangles
1	cucumber, peeled and cut into ½-inch half moons
½	red onion, thinly sliced into half-moons
8	ounces feta cheese, cut into small cubes (about 2 cups) or thin triangles
¼	cup pitted black oil-cured olives
2	tablespoons olive oil
1	teaspoon red wine vinegar
	Freshly ground pepper
2	tablespoons fresh mint, thinly sliced into ribbons

1. ARRANGE THE WATERMELON CHUNKS or triangles in a large shallow bowl or serving plate.

2. LAYER THE TOP of the watermelon with the cucumber, then the red onion slices, feta, and olives. Drizzle with the oil and vinegar and pepper.

3. SPRINKLE THE MINT over the salad and serve.

Southwestern Slaw

This is a crunchy, mayo-free way to think about coleslaw. The lime and honey temper the bite of the chile powder, and it's a refreshing side to grilled or roasted chicken, fish, or pork tenderloin.

Jicama tastes a bit like a cross between a water chestnut and an apple. It's terrific to snack on—consider it a fresh alternative to the usual celery. It keeps well in the veggie bin.

SERVES 6

NUTRITION PER SERVING:
CALORIES 151, TOTAL FAT 4g, SODIUM 29mg, SUGARS 10g

1   large jicama, peeled and finely shredded
1   (14-ounce) bag coleslaw mix
¼   cup finely chopped fresh cilantro
     Zest and juice of 1 lime
     Zest and juice of 1 orange
2   teaspoons ancho chile powder
2   tablespoons honey
1   tablespoon canola oil
     Salt and freshly ground black pepper

1. IN A LARGE BOWL, combine the shredded jicama, coleslaw mix, and cilantro, mixing well.

2. IN A SMALL BOWL, make the dressing: Whisk together the lime zest and juice, the orange zest and juice, ancho chile powder, honey, oil, and salt and pepper to taste.

3. POUR THE DRESSING over the jicama mixture and let sit at room temperature for about 15 minutes to absorb the dressing.

Sweet Potato Gratin

Gratins give you the best of everything—the veggies you need, plus a bit of creamy texture and a golden crust, all in one package. This version uses sweet potatoes, but you can swap Yukon golds or the more familiar Idahos. Add a sliced apple for a spectacular holiday side dish. Here we've cut the calories by replacing the usual cream and butter with a mixture of cream and stock and thickened it with flour. Don't miss our bonus chipotle variation below.

SERVES 4

NUTRITION PER SERVING:
CALORIES 238, TOTAL FAT 8g, SODIUM 927mg, SUGARS 7g

⅔	cup low-sodium, reduced-fat chicken stock
⅓	cup heavy cream
1½	pounds sweet potatoes, peeled and thinly sliced
1½	teaspoons salt
1	tablespoon all-purpose flour
2	tablespoons finely grated Parmesan cheese

1. **PREHEAT THE OVEN** to 375°F and place the rack in the center.

2. **COMBINE THE CHICKEN STOCK** and cream in a measuring cup. In an 8×8-inch Pyrex baking dish, layer about one-third of the sweet potato slices over the bottom of the dish. Sprinkle with ½ teaspoon salt and half of the flour, and pour over about one-third of the stock-cream mixture.

3. **LAYER ANOTHER THIRD** of the potato slices on top, sprinkle with ½ teaspoon salt and the remaining flour, and pour over half of the remaining stock-cream mixture. Layer the remaining potato slices on top, sprinkle with the remaining ½ teaspoon salt, and pour over the rest of the stock-cream mixture. Sprinkle evenly with the cheese.

(continued)

4. COVER WITH ALUMINUM FOIL and bake 35 minutes. Uncover and bake until the liquid has reduced (the gratin will not be entirely dry) and the top is lightly browned, 35 to 40 more minutes. Let stand about 15 minutes before serving.

VARIATION: Blend 1 teaspoon chipotle chile in adobo sauce with the chicken stock and cream in a blender or food processor. Layer and bake the gratin as above.

Creamed Spinach

Here's the side dish everyone loves, on the lighter side. You can even cut out a tablespoon of butter and barely miss it if you are on a tight calorie or fat count. Try to keep fresh nutmeg in your spice cabinet; it really makes a difference.

SERVES 4

NUTRITION PER SERVING:
CALORIES 165, TOTAL FAT 9g, SODIUM 246mg, SUGARS 5g

1   cup skim milk
3   tablespoons unsalted butter
1   onion, finely chopped
3   tablespoons all-purpose flour
2   bags (7 to 9 ounces each) baby spinach
¼   teaspoon salt
¼   teaspoon pepper
⅛   teaspoon freshly grated nutmeg

1. MICROWAVE THE MILK on High until warm, about 1 minute. Meanwhile, melt the butter in a large skillet over medium heat. Add the onion and cook, stirring occasionally, until golden and tender, about 5 minutes. Stir in the flour and cook, stirring constantly, for 2 minutes. Continue stirring and add the warm milk in a slow, steady stream. Bring the mixture to a boil, stirring, and continue cooking and stirring until thickened and completely smooth, about 3 minutes.

2. STIR IN THE SPINACH until it wilts and turns bright green, about 2 minutes. Season with the salt, pepper, and nutmeg and serve immediately.

Stuffed Peppers with Orzo and Olives

Keep a rainbow of peppers in your veggie bin for snacking, throwing into stir-fries, or for this Greek-inspired stuffed delight. Look for whole wheat orzo for a hearty accent, although the plain will work well too. You can add ⅓ cup feta cheese for a main-course supper along with our Carrot Soup with a Kick (page 123).

SERVES 4

NUTRITION PER SERVING:
CALORIES 200, TOTAL FAT 7g, SODIUM 430mg, SUGARS 9g

½   cup whole wheat orzo
1   tablespoon olive oil
1   onion, diced
¼   teaspoon salt
1   zucchini, diced
1   tomato, cored and diced
¼   cup chopped pitted Kalamata olives
2   red bell peppers, stemmed, seeded, and halved

1. **PREHEAT THE OVEN** to 425°F. Line a 13×9-inch baking dish with aluminum foil.

2. **COOK THE ORZO** until al dente according to package directions.

(continued)

3. MEANWHILE, heat the oil in a 12-inch skillet over medium heat. Add the onion, season with salt, and cook, stirring occasionally, until tender, about 4 minutes. Add the zucchini and cook, stirring occasionally, just until tender, about 3 minutes. Remove from the heat, and stir in the tomato, olives, and orzo.

4. DIVIDE THE ORZO MIXTURE among the peppers and arrange in a single layer in the prepared pan. Bake until the peppers are tender, about 25 minutes.

Chopped "Taco" Salad

Those taco bowl salads are yummy but laden with hidden calories. We've turned this salad upside down, mixing crisp romaine with protein-packed beans and cheese and a few baked tortilla chips for crunch. A bright buttermilk dressing pulls it all together. For a main-course dinner salad, add 2 cups shredded chicken breast or fish. And try our ranch dressing on grilled meats, fish, and veggies too.

SERVES 4

NUTRITION PER SERVING:
CALORIES 202, TOTAL FAT 9g, SODIUM 539mg, SUGARS 4g

For the dressing:
⅓ cup light mayonnaise
⅓ cup reduced-fat buttermilk
2 garlic cloves, finely chopped
¼ cup finely chopped fresh cilantro
2 tablespoons thinly sliced scallions
Zest and juice of ½ lime
¼ teaspoon salt
⅛ teaspoon freshly ground pepper
Pinch of cayenne or ancho chile powder, or more to taste

For the salad:
10 ounces romaine lettuce or 2 romaine hearts
1 (15-ounce) can low-sodium black beans, drained and well rinsed and dried
⅓ cup shredded pepper Jack or Cheddar cheese
2 tomatoes, chopped
8 baked fat-free tortilla chips

1. **TO MAKE THE DRESSING,** combine all the dressing ingredients in a small bowl and whisk until creamy.

2. **FOR THE SALAD,** chop the romaine into ribbons and place on a platter or individual serving plates. Top with the black beans, cheese, and tomatoes. Drizzle on the dressing and top with tortilla chips.

Cheddar Melts

Grilled cheese, but a better-for-you version! Try to find a true dark pumpernickel, like the Mestemacher brand. Make half for an after-school snack or for a light supper along with any of our soups, like the Hearty Vegetable and Lentil Soup (page 125).

SERVES 4

NUTRITION PER SERVING:
CALORIES 256, TOTAL FAT 5g, SODIUM 649mg, SUGARS 6g

1   Granny Smith apple, cored, with skin
1   teaspoon unsalted butter
2   tablespoons honey mustard
8   slices pumpernickel or dark wheat bread
      Cooking spray
8   thin slices low-fat Cheddar cheese

1. SLICE ¼ INCH off both ends of the apple. Cut the remaining apple into 4 slices.

2. MELT THE BUTTER in a large nonstick pan over medium heat and add the apple slices. Cook for 1 to 2 minutes per side until they are golden brown and slightly soft.

3. REMOVE THE PAN from the heat, transfer the apples to a plate, and keep warm.

4. SPREAD THE MUSTARD on 4 slices of bread.

5. LIGHTLY SPRAY the same pan with cooking spray and turn the heat to medium-high.

6. WORKING IN BATCHES, add 4 slices of bread, mustard side up. Top each slice of bread with a slice of cheese, and top the cheese with the apple. Top the apples with the remaining cheese and bread.

7. USING A SPATULA, press down on the sandwiches and cover the pan with a lid and cook for 1 minute. When the bottom cheese has melted, flip the sandwich, press down, and continue to cook about 1 minute longer, until the bottom cheese has melted.

8. REMOVE FROM THE PAN, slice on the diagonal, and serve immediately.

Creamy Corn Chowder

Smoky bacon and creamy corn come together in a flash for a hearty soup for any season. Pair this with half of a Cheddar Melt (page 138) or our Chopped "Taco" Salad (page 137) for a big lunch or light supper.

SERVES 4

NUTRITION PER SERVING:
CALORIES 104, TOTAL FAT 2g, SODIUM 174mg, SUGARS 6g

1   strip bacon, chopped
1   sweet onion, diced
1   Yukon gold potato, diced
5   cups water
3   ears corn on the cob (or 3 cups frozen corn, defrosted)
½   teaspoon chopped fresh thyme, or ¼ teaspoon dried
¼   teaspoon salt
¼   teaspoon pepper

1. COOK THE BACON in a 4-quart saucepan over medium heat, stirring occasionally, until crisp and golden brown, about 3 minutes. Remove the bacon with a slotted spoon and drain on paper towels; keep the rendered fat in the pan.

2. ADD THE ONION to the pan and cook, stirring occasionally, until golden brown and tender, about 7 minutes. Add the potato and water, bring to a simmer, and cook until tender, about 15 minutes.

3. MEANWHILE, cut the corn kernels off the cobs with a large knife. Using the large holes of a box grater, grate the cobs over a bowl to extract the juices. Add the kernels and corn juices to the saucepan and simmer until the corn is tender, about 5 minutes.

4. TRANSFER 3 CUPS of the soup to the bowl of a blender or food processor and carefully puree. Pour the puree back into the saucepan and heat through on low heat, about 2 minutes. Stir in the thyme, salt, and pepper. Garnish with the bacon and serve.

Joanne

Joanne was a busy working mom who was relying way too much on her microwave and store-bought caloric (and costly) dinners to feed her family. She needed a bit more confidence in the kitchen, and found the simple CYT recipes a big comfort.

"I had a difficult time getting motivated. I wondered how I was going to do this and was thinking it was a huge daunting task. I then shrunk the tasks to day-to-day challenges instead of month-to-month. I also found shopping for healthy foods made better choice decisions for on-the-go eating. I began to be very good at reading labels, and once I perfected the brand, location of store, and location in the supermarkets, it made shopping much less daunting.

"Initially, I had to make the time to get the ingredients. Give me the tools and I can do the work kind of thing. *CYT* ingredients will be the staple items in my kitchen and I look forward to using them on an ongoing basis for future recipes.

"And now that I've dropped two dress sizes I feel younger, skinnier, smarter, healthier, and sexier!"

Dessert

Give up chocolate? Live without dessert? There's no need. Remember, we've said it before and we're happy to repeat it: Yes, you can have your cake and eat it too!

Just not with all the fat and calories, please. We think you deserve dessert, so we've slashed the calories and fat for you with some creative twists on your favorites. Go on, take a bite!

Many of these can be made ahead, with minimal prep work. In fact, many are even more delicious the next day.

No Machine Ice Cream

Here's a way to satisfy that craving without the guilt and another appliance. The best thing is that this is a base recipe: Mix in cherries or strawberries, chopped nuts, some instant espresso powder, or even half of our Low-Fat Granola Bar (page 37). The dramatic change here is in the fat content—less than half that of the leading brands of light ice cream.

SERVES 8

NUTRITION PER SERVING:
CALORIES 239, TOTAL FAT 5g, SODIUM 93mg, SUGARS 32g

1   (12-ounce) can low-fat evaporated milk
1   (14-ounce) can fat-free sweetened condensed milk
1   cup half and half
1   teaspoon vanilla extract
½   cup unsweetened cocoa powder, sifted

PUT ALL THE INGREDIENTS in a large bowl and whisk to combine. Pour into a freezer-safe bowl or a loaf pan, which makes scooping it simpler. Press plastic wrap onto the surface to prevent crystallization. Freeze for 6 hours or overnight.

Chocolate Volcano Cakes

Here's a four-star dessert, in all its molten glory! Super fast and super impressive, here's the cake we promised you—warm, deep, dark chocolate with a soft center. We've cut the fat and calories so you can savor it with a whisper of whipped cream. This batch can be easily doubled to make a full tray of 12 for entertaining.

SERVES 6

NUTRITION PER CAKE:
CALORIES 298, TOTAL FAT 19g, SODIUM 116mg, SUGARS 22g

	Cooking spray
	Cocoa powder, for muffin tins
2½	tablespoons unsalted butter, at room temperature
⅓	cup granulated sugar
2	large eggs
1	egg white
⅓	cup all-purpose flour
¼	teaspoon salt
6	ounces bittersweet chocolate, melted
	Confectioners' sugar, for serving
¼	cup heavy cream, for serving

1. PREHEAT THE OVEN to 400°F.

2. SPRAY 6 CUPS of a standard muffin tin with cooking spray. Dust with cocoa powder and tap out the excess. Place on a baking sheet.

3. USING A STANDING MIXER fitted with the paddle attachment or with the beaters of an electric hand mixer, cream the butter and granulated sugar until fluffy, about 1 minute.

4. ADD THE EGGS and egg white one at a time, beating well after each addition.

(continued)

5. LOWER THE SPEED to low and mix in the flour and salt until just combined. Add the chocolate and mix, again, until just combined. Divide the batter evenly among the prepared muffin cups.

6. BAKE JUST UNTIL the tops of the cakes no longer jiggle when the pan is lightly shaken, 8 to 10 minutes. Remove from the oven, place on a cooking rack, and let rest for 5 minutes.

7. MEANWHILE, using a whisk or electric mixer, whip the cream.

8. WITH THE HELP of a small offset spatula or spoon, invert the cakes onto serving plates; the bottom will now become the top. Don't worry if they crack slightly. Just dust with confectioners' sugar and serve with a dollop of whipped cream.

> **TIP:** Melt the chocolate in the microwave, checking after 30-second intervals. Mix after each check as chips often keep their shape even when melted.

Cherry Vanilla
Rice Pudding

This is a comforting dessert that's charming enough for company but can easily be put together from your pantry. If you don't have dried cherries try currants, raisins, or dried blueberries and add ½ teaspoon cinnamon instead of the almond extract. We love this served warm for a cozy winter dessert or chilled for a refreshing treat.

SERVES 6

NUTRITION PER SERVING:
CALORIES 196, TOTAL FAT 2g, SODIUM 152mg, SUGARS 23g

¼   cup dried cherries
4½   cups low-fat (1%) milk
⅔   cup long-grain white rice
⅓   cup sugar
1   teaspoon orange zest
    Pinch of salt
½   teaspoon vanilla extract
½   teaspoon almond extract

1. **PLACE THE DRIED FRUIT** in a small bowl, cover with hot water, and set aside.

2. **IN A MEDIUM SAUCEPAN** set over medium heat, combine the milk, rice, sugar, orange zest, and salt and bring to a simmer, stirring frequently. Reduce the heat to low and simmer gently until the rice is very tender and the pudding is creamy, stirring occasionally, for about 35 to 40 minutes.

3. **REMOVE THE PAN** from the heat. Drain the dried fruit and mix into the rice along with the vanilla and almond extracts. Transfer to individual ramekins or a large serving bowl. Serve warm or refrigerate and serve chilled.

Dessert Pizza

Pie dough is filled with fat and calories. Pizza dough is a super substitute as it's usually fat free. Keep a stash of store-bought dough in the freezer and you can defrost it overnight in the fridge for an easy weekend dessert. Experiment with different fruits too—try apples and raisins, pears and blue cheese with a few hazelnuts . . . or all berries! Brushing the dough with milk and sprinkling with sugar pumps up the sweetness and makes the crust sparkle.

SERVES 8 TO 10

NUTRITION PER SERVING:
CALORIES 168, TOTAL FAT 1g, SODIUM 121mg, SUGARS 20g

½   pound pizza dough
4   large peaches, sliced
2   pints berries
3   tablespoons all-purpose flour
½   cup plus 1 tablespoon sugar
2   teaspoons skim milk

1. **PREHEAT THE OVEN** to 375°F.

2. **LINE A BAKING SHEET** with lightly greased parchment paper.

3. **STRETCH THE DOUGH** into a circle, directly onto the baking pan, pressing and gently stretching to fill as much of the pan as possible. It will be about 11 inches in diameter.

4. **IN A MEDIUM BOWL,** mix the fruit with flour and ½ cup sugar. Place the fruit mixture over the center of the crust and evenly arrange. Leave a 1-inch border of dough. Pull the edges of the dough up against the fruit to form a rustic crust. Brush the outer crust with milk and sprinkle with the remaining tablespoon of sugar.

5. **BAKE THE PIZZA** for 30 to 40 minutes, until the crust is crisp and bubbling and the fruit is softened and nicely caramelized. Serve warm.

White Chocolate Delight

White chocolate lovers, rejoice! This dessert is sophisticated and simple and an impressive fast comfort food for your friends. You can also top with raspberries or blueberries instead of the strawberries.

 The trick to not burning the chocolate while microwaving is to stir well after each 30-second interval because the chocolate often holds its shape even while melted, especially if you are using chips. Make sure you let the chocolate and cream cool so you have a smooth, creamy dessert. This can be made a day or so ahead; just make the fruit topping the day you are serving and add right before serving.

SERVES 6

NUTRITION PER SERVING:
CALORIES 264, TOTAL FAT 14g, SODIUM 56mg, SUGARS 22g

6   ounces white chocolate, finely chopped
¼   cup heavy cream
2   cups low-fat (2%) Greek-style yogurt
½   teaspoon vanilla extract
1½   cups sliced strawberries
2   teaspoons sugar

1. IN A MEDIUM BOWL, combine the white chocolate and cream, microwave for 30-second intervals, and stir until melted, about 1 minute. If still not melted, return and continue to melt for 30-second intervals, stirring well each time before returning to the microwave. Transfer to a medium bowl and allow to cool thoroughly, about 30 minutes.

2. WHISK THE YOGURT and vanilla into the white chocolate mixture until smooth, and spoon into serving glasses or bowls. Press plastic wrap over the surface and refrigerate until set, about 2 hours.

3. MEANWHILE, combine the strawberries and sugar in a bowl and keep refrigerated.

4. TOP THE WHITE CHOCOLATE mixture with a few spoonfuls of the strawberries and serve immediately.

Brown Sugar Kisses

We love meringues—they are simple to make, you only need egg whites and sugar, and best of all, they're fat free! We've switched things up by using brown sugar, and while these cookies won't be the usual snowy white, they have an addictive caramel flavor you'll love. You can also bake one large meringue and top with berries and a bit of whipped cream.

MAKES 30 KISSES

NUTRITION PER COOKIE:
CALORIES 11, TOTAL FAT less than 1g, SODIUM 10mg, SUGARS 2g

3	egg whites
	Pinch of salt
½	cup light brown sugar
½	teaspoon vanilla extract

1. **PREHEAT THE OVEN** to 225°F.

2. **LINE 2 BAKING TRAYS** with parchment paper or a silicone sheet.

3. **IN A LARGE STANDING MIXER** fitted with a whisk, or a handheld mixer, beat the egg whites and salt on high speed until soft peaks form. Add the sugar slowly while beating, a few spoonfuls at a time, until the meringue is stiff and shiny, about 3 to 5 minutes. Add the vanilla and beat to combine.

4. **USING A LARGE TABLESPOON,** drop the meringue onto the prepared baking sheet in the shape of kisses about 2 inches apart. Or cut the corner off a large plastic bag, fill with meringue, and squeeze out the kisses. Bake for about 1 hour and 15 minutes.

5. **TURN THE OVEN OFF** and keep the door ajar. Let cool for 1 hour in the oven. Store in a tin or wrap loosely in aluminum foil; do not store in plastic wrap or glass or the cookies will become soggy.

Chocolate Cheesecake Cupcakes

These darling cupcakes deliver the best of both worlds: chocolate and a cheesecake, all in one delectable bite. Try using white chocolate chips in place of the usual semisweet for a black-and-white version.

MAKES 12 MINI CUPCAKES

NUTRITION PER CUPCAKE:
CALORIES 114, TOTAL FAT 6g, SODIUM 83mg, SUGARS 11g

- ½ cup unsweetened cocoa powder
- ¼ cup all-purpose flour
- ¼ teaspoon baking powder
- ⅛ teaspoon salt
- ½ cup granulated sugar
- 3 tablespoons vegetable oil
- 1 large egg white
- 1 teaspoon pure vanilla extract
- 2 tablespoons chocolate chips
- ½ cup whipped low-fat cream cheese
- 1 tablespoon confectioners' sugar

1. **PREHEAT THE OVEN** to 350°F. Line 12 cups of a mini muffin tin with paper liners.

2. **WHISK TOGETHER** the cocoa powder, flour, baking powder, and salt in a small bowl until well combined. In a large bowl, whisk together the granulated sugar, oil, egg white, and vanilla until well blended. Add the cocoa powder mixture to the sugar mixture and stir until combined. Stir in the chocolate chips.

3. **DIVIDE THE BATTER** among the muffin cups. Bake until a toothpick inserted into the center of one comes out slightly wet, about 20 minutes. Cool in the pan on a wire rack until completely cooled.

4. **MEANWHILE,** beat the cream cheese and confectioners' sugar together in a small bowl until smooth and fluffy. When ready to serve, top each cupcake with a dollop of cream cheese.

Meringue Clouds

This is a most romantic dessert, and it's fat free! Sophisticated yet simple, it can be made a day ahead. You probably have most of the ingredients already on hand. Don't worry about making perfect rounds—imperfect "clouds" are still delicious!

SERVES 4

NUTRITION PER SERVING:
CALORIES 135, TOTAL FAT less than 1g, SODIUM 42mg, SUGARS 28g

3	large egg whites
¼	teaspoon pure vanilla extract
	Pinch of salt
⅓	cup sugar
1½	cups frozen raspberries, thawed
2	tablespoons honey

1. **LINE A 13×9-INCH** baking dish with plastic wrap and set aside.

2. **USING A STANDING MIXER** or a handheld mixer, whisk the egg whites, vanilla, and salt on high speed until soft peaks form. Continue to whisk and gradually add the sugar a few tablespoons at a time until stiff peaks form. The mixture should be glossy.

3. **TO POACH** the 4 meringues, fill a large skillet with 1 inch of water. Place the pan over high heat and bring the water to a simmer. Reduce the heat to medium-low so the water does not bubble.

4. **DIP A LARGE SPOON** in cold water and remove a quarter of the egg white mixture. Smooth the top with a rubber spatula and gently slide the meringue off the spoon into the skillet. Repeat with the remaining meringues. Poach 4 minutes on one side. Gently turn over the meringues and continue to poach for about 3 more minutes, until slightly firm to the touch.

(continued)

5. REMOVE EACH MERINGUE with a slotted spoon, pat the bottom of the spoon on a paper towel to blot any extra water, and transfer to the prepared pan.

6. COVER THE PAN with plastic wrap, and refrigerate at least 30 minutes or overnight.

7. FOR THE SAUCE, combine the raspberries and honey in a blender or food processor. Blend on high speed until smooth, and pour through a strainer to remove the seeds.

8. DRIZZLE THE SAUCE evenly over 4 plates and top each with a meringue.

Chocolate Espresso Cookies

Cookies with a kick! Espresso and chocolate come together for a grown-up treat that's easy to make and low in calories and fat. If you love almonds you can add ¼ teaspoon almond extract.

MAKES 24 COOKIES

NUTRITION PER COOKIE:
CALORIES 69, TOTAL FAT 2g, SODIUM 17mg, SUGARS 10g

    Cooking spray
2¼ cups sifted confectioners' sugar
6   tablespoons unsweetened cocoa powder
1   tablespoon instant espresso powder
¼   cup all-purpose flour
¼   teaspoon salt
3   large egg whites
1   teaspoon vanilla extract
½   cup finely ground almonds
1½ ounces bittersweet chocolate, finely chopped

1. **PREHEAT THE OVEN** to 325°F.

2. **LINE 2 BAKING SHEETS** with silicone sheets or parchment paper. Lightly spray with cooking spray if using parchment.

3. **IN A LARGE BOWL** using a whisk, combine the confectioners' sugar, cocoa and espresso powders, flour, and salt. Beat in the egg whites one at a time with an electric mixer on low speed. Add the vanilla and beat for 1½ minutes on high speed, scraping down the sides of the bowl several times. Fold in the nuts and chocolate until evenly incorporated.

4. **SPOON THE DOUGH** by heaping tablespoonfuls onto the prepared baking sheets about 2 inches apart.

5. **BAKE ABOUT 15 TO 17 MINUTES.** The cookies will look shiny and firm

6. **LET COOL ON THE PAN** for 5 minutes, then transfer the entire sheet of paper to a cooling rack before removing the cookies from the paper to serve.

Raspberry Lemon Tea Cake

This is a lower-fat version of a pound cake by a fabulous baker and food writer, Dorie Greenspan. Feel free to play with it even more—add a lemon glaze, or swap blueberries for the raspberries. You can also omit the fruit and add a splash of vanilla and ¼ cup mini chocolate chips. It freezes well and is delicious when toasted.

SERVES 10

NUTRITION PER SERVING:
CALORIES 219, TOTAL FAT 9g, SODIUM 139mg, SUGARS 16g

	Cooking spray
1½	cups all-purpose flour
2	teaspoons baking powder
	Pinch of salt
¾	cup low-fat (2%) Greek-style yogurt
2	large eggs
¼	teaspoon pure vanilla extract
¾	cup sugar
	Zest of 1 lemon
1	cup raspberries
⅓	cup canola oil

1. **PREHEAT THE OVEN** to 350°F.

2. **LIGHTLY SPRAY** an 8½ × 4½-inch loaf pan.

3. **IN A SMALL BOWL,** whisk together the flour, baking powder, and salt.

4. **IN A MEDIUM BOWL,** whisk the yogurt, eggs, vanilla, sugar, and lemon zest. Lightly whisk in the dry ingredients until incorporated. Using a rubber spatula, fold in the raspberries and slowly pour in the oil, folding it into the batter. Transfer the batter to the baking pan.

5. **BAKE FOR 50 TO 55 MINUTES,** or until it is golden and starts to come away from the sides of the pan. A toothpick inserted into the center of the cake should come out clean.

6. **COOL ON A RACK** for 5 minutes, then run a knife along the edges of the pan to loosen the cake. Flip the cake out of the pan to cool right side up.

Fudgy Brownies

You can never have too many brownie recipes! This version has a bit of caramel flavor from the brown sugar. These are great to pack for that on-the-run snack or school lunch treat without the guilt.

MAKES 18 BROWNIES

NUTRITION PER BROWNIE:
CALORIES 56, TOTAL FAT 3g, SODIUM 23mg, SUGARS 4g

	Cooking spray
¼	cup unsweetened cocoa powder, preferably Dutch process, plus extra for the pan
½	teaspoon baking powder
⅓	cup all-purpose flour
3	tablespoons vegetable or canola oil
½	cup light brown sugar
2	large eggs, beaten
1	teaspoon vanilla extract

1. **PREHEAT THE OVEN** to 350°F.

2. **LIGHTLY SPRAY** an 8×8-inch baking pan with cooking spray and then coat the pan with cocoa powder.

3. **IN A SMALL BOWL,** whisk together the cocoa powder, baking powder, and flour. Set aside.

4. **IN A LARGE BOWL,** using a whisk, combine the oil and sugar. Add the eggs and vanilla and whisk until well blended. Gently mix in the flour mixture and transfer the batter to the pan. Bake for 13 to 15 minutes, taking care not to overbake. A toothpick inserted into the center should not be completely dry. A few moist crumbs on the pick means you will have fudgy brownies.

Brown Butter Cobbler

Kids and grown-ups are amazed by this lighter cobbler. Don't worry that the method seems backward—the batter will rise to the top like a traditional cobbler. Browning the butter adds a nutty flavor so you can use less butter than usual. Try any combination of your favorite stone fruit or berries or even sliced apples or pears.

SERVES 6

NUTRITION PER SERVING:
CALORIES 326, TOTAL FAT 10g, SODIUM 306mg, SUGARS 37g

2½ cups nectarines or peaches, sliced, skin left on
    (about 3 to 4 large, about 1 pound)
½   cup blueberries
½   cup plus 2 tablespoons granulated sugar
5   tablespoons unsalted butter
1   cup all-purpose flour
1   tablespoon baking powder
¼   teaspoon ground cinnamon
    Pinch of salt
¾   cup low-fat (1%) milk
½   teaspoon vanilla extract
¼   cup firmly packed light brown sugar

1. **PREHEAT THE OVEN** to 350°F.

2. **IN A MEDIUM BOWL,** toss the fruit with 2 tablespoons of the granulated sugar and set aside.

3. **PLACE THE BUTTER** in an 8×8-inch square baking dish and bake for 4 to 5 minutes, until the butter is melted and turns a light nut brown. Remove the pan from the oven and carefully set aside.

(continued)

4. IN A MEDIUM BOWL, stir together the flour, baking powder, the remaining ½ cup granulated sugar, cinnamon, and salt. Slowly pour in the milk and vanilla and stir. Carefully spread the batter over the melted butter.

5. EVENLY ARRANGE THE FRUIT over the batter. Sprinkle the entire surface with the brown sugar.

6. BAKE THE COBBLER for 40 to 45 minutes, until the top turns golden brown, rotating the pan midway through baking. Serve immediately.

Tiramisù

We can't leave an Italian restaurant without ordering tiramisù, but now it comes home without all the fat and calories. Store-bought ladyfingers are great to keep on hand too; use them for a faster version of our Strawberry Shortcake (page 169).

SERVES 4

NUTRITION PER SERVING:
CALORIES 145, TOTAL FAT 11g, SODIUM 33mg, SUGARS 3g

¼   cup heavy cream
1   tablespoon mascarpone cheese
1   ounce brewed espresso
1   teaspoon Marsala wine
4   ladyfingers, cut in half
1   ounce bittersweet chocolate

1. WHISK TOGETHER the cream and mascarpone in a large bowl until stiff peaks form. Combine the espresso and Marsala in a shallow dish.

2. SOAK 2 LADYFINGER HALVES in the espresso mixture until wet but not falling apart and arrange side by side in a 4-ounce ramekin or serving dish. Repeat with the remaining ladyfingers. Divide the cream mixture among the ramekins. Cover with plastic wrap and refrigerate until very cold and set, about 4 hours.

3. WHEN READY TO SERVE, uncover. Using a fine grater or vegetable peeler, shave the chocolate over the top of the dessert.

Mocha Mousse

This is a glamorous dessert that looks super cool when served in espresso cups or shot glasses. Use the best-quality chocolate you can find—you'll taste the difference. If you prefer semisweet, omit the sugar. Keep in mind this recipe uses uncooked eggs, so it's not the thing to serve pregnant women or small kids. For a change of pace, omit the espresso and add a splash of orange juice or orange liqueur instead, and top with orange zest.

SERVES 4

NUTRITION PER SERVING:

CALORIES 86, TOTAL FAT 11g, SODIUM 36mg, SUGARS 9g

3   ounces dark chocolate, melted
1-ounce shot of espresso, at room temperature
2   large eggs, separated
1   teaspoon sugar

1. IN A LARGE BOWL, using a whisk, combine the chocolate and espresso. (If very warm, set aside to cool slightly.)

2. IN ANOTHER LARGE BOWL, using a whisk or handheld mixer, whisk the egg whites, gradually adding the sugar until stiff peaks form.

3. BEAT THE EGG YOLKS into the chocolate mixture. Using a spatula, mix a third of the egg white mixture into the chocolate to lighten the base. Gently fold in the remaining egg whites. Carefully, evenly divide the mousse into 4 espresso cups or small ramekins. Refrigerate at least 3 hours or overnight.

Strawberry Shortcake

Perfect for parties and picnics or to brighten a rainy day, our Strawberry Shortcake is less than 200 calories! How did we do it? Sweetened, thick low-fat Greek yogurt, fragrant with lemon peel, is our smart swap for the usual whipped cream.

SERVES 4

NUTRITION PER SERVING:
CALORIES 181, TOTAL FAT 7g, SODIUM 201mg, SUGARS 10g

½	cup all-purpose flour
1	teaspoon baking powder
⅛	teaspoon salt
3	teaspoons sugar
2	tablespoons unsalted butter, cut into small pieces
¼	cup low-fat milk
½	cup low-fat plain Greek yogurt
1	teaspoon grated lemon zest
1	pound strawberries, hulled and quartered

1. PREHEAT THE OVEN to 425°F. Line a baking sheet with parchment paper.

2. COMBINE THE FLOUR, baking powder, salt, and 1 teaspoon sugar in a large bowl. Using a pastry blender or your fingertips, cut the butter into the flour mixture until the mixture resembles coarse crumbs with a few pea-sized pieces remaining. Add milk and stir just until the mixture forms a shaggy dough.

3. DIVIDE THE DOUGH into 4 pieces in the bowl and drop onto the prepared pan. Bake until golden brown, about 15 minutes.

4. MEANWHILE, combine the yogurt, lemon zest, and 1 teaspoon sugar. In another bowl, combine the strawberries and remaining teaspoon of sugar.

5. LET THE SHORTCAKES cool 5 minutes on a wire rack. Split each and sandwich with yogurt and strawberries.

Panna Cotta

The recipe title means "cooked cream" in Italian and translates to smooth deliciousness minus the fat in our version. We've cleverly swapped the usual heavy cream with tangy buttermilk and some half-and-half for richness. You can drizzle this with a bit of honey for a gorgeous presentation. Try making these in heart-shaped silicone molds for romantic dinners.

SERVES 4

NUTRITION PER SERVING:
CALORIES 104, TOTAL FAT 4g, SODIUM 77mg, SUGARS 12g

1   teaspoon unflavored gelatin
1   tablespoon water
½   cup half-and-half
3   tablespoons sugar
1   cup low-fat buttermilk
½   teaspoon vanilla extract

1. SPRINKLE THE GELATIN over the water in a small bowl and let soften for 5 minutes.

2. MEANWHILE, combine the half-and-half and sugar in a small sauce-pan and warm over medium heat, stirring to dissolve the sugar. Remove from the heat and stir in the gelatin mixture until it dissolves. Cool completely.

3. STIR THE BUTTERMILK and vanilla into the gelatin mixture. Divide among four 5-ounce ramekins or serving dishes. Refrigerate, uncovered, until the panna cotta is set, about 8 hours.

4. RUN A THIN, SHARP KNIFE around the sides of each ramekin to loosen the panna cotta. One at a time, place bottom of each ramekin in 1 inch of hot water for 30 to 45 seconds; immediately invert the ramekin onto the serving plate. Remove the ramekin and serve.

Tara   BEFORE: Size 12   AFTER: Size 10; lost 6 pounds

Tara, a young girl who was about to set out on her adult life, needed better habits. An aspiring model, she was desperate to take off the pounds that were holding her back.

"*Cook Yourself Thin* is the best way I've found to look at food and eating. Diets never work because they are restrictive and temporary, but with the *Cook Yourself Thin* philosophy, I learned how to change my lifestyle!

"I now make substitutions for healthier ingredients, and am enjoying how I look and feel. It's so easy, because it's not any more work than cooking a fattening meal, and it doesn't taste any less good either—the only thing you miss are the extra calories.

"My tips: Using fat-free whipped cream to make a treat à la mode, making a side of veggies to eat with lunch and dinner (the veggies help fill you up without adding fat and too many calories), and if you're busy like me, making large portions of your favorite *CYT* meals and freezing the extra so you can just pop it in the microwave at work!"

Menus

First things first. *Cook Yourself Thin Faster* is not a diet.

The whole point of *Cook Yourself Thin* is that diets don't work in the long term—after all, who can stick to a rigid plan indefinitely? Instead, we all have to learn to take control of the food we cook and eat, stay flexible, and accept that our tastes change according to our moods, the seasons—even which side of the bed we got out of! Sometimes you just can't bear another salad and nothing but a big bowl of pasta will do. Here are some great ideas to keep you from getting bored, to keep your family on board, and for cooking yourself thin while you entertain.

BRUNCH

Violet Morning Smoothie 34 *or* Almondy Joy 36

Spicy Mary 41

Eggs Italian Style 22 *or* Asparagus and Goat Cheese Quiche 29 *or* Mini Blueberry Muffins 32

Sautéed Corn Cakes with Smoked Salmon 59

New Greek Salad 128

Raspberry Lemon Tea Cake 160

GIRLS' NIGHT

Pineapple Mojitos 61

White Pizza with Roasted Mushrooms 63

Pizza with Sweet Peppers and Goat Cheese 65

Asian Chicken Salad 77

No Machine Ice Cream 145 *or* Fudgy Brownies 162

ROMANTIC DINNER FOR TWO

Blush Sangria 50

Stuffed Mushrooms 47 *or* Carrot Soup with a Kick 123

Pork with Apples 84 *or* Mussels 98 *or* Swordfish Arrabiata 107

Creamed Spinach 133

Chocolate Volcano Cakes 147 *or* Brown Sugar Kisses 155 *or* Meringue Clouds 157 *or* Panna Cotta 170

HOLIDAY SPREAD

Spinach Dip 48 *or* Roasted Chickpeas with Rosemary 53

Turkey Meatloaf with Dried Cranberries 88 *or* Cod Saltimbocca 102

Sweet Potato Gratin 131 *or* Creamed Spinach 133 *or* Carrot Soup with a Kick 123

Cherry Vanilla Rice Pudding 149 *or* Mocha Mousse 66 *or* White Chocolate
Delight 152

PICNIC BASKET

Seven-Layer Dip 67

Oven-Fried Chicken with Cinnamon Spice 92 *or* BBQ Salmon 104 *or* Flank Steak
with Indian Salsa 79

Red, White, and Blue Potato Salad 121 *or* Southwestern Slaw 130

Strawberry Shortcake 169 *or* Brown Butter Cobbler 163 *or* Fudgy Brownies 162

TAKEOUT MADE IN

Hot Wings 57

Pork Tacos 75 *or* Orange Beef 81 *or* Cashew Chicken 86 *or* Fish and Chips 111

Chopped "Taco" Salad 137 *or* Cheese "Fries" 127

Dessert Pizza 150 *or* No Machine Ice Cream 145

COMFORT FOOD

Creamy Corn Chowder 140 *or* Hearty Vegetable and Lentil Soup 125 *or*
Cheddar Melts 138 *or* Creamed Spinach 133 *or* Cheese Biscuits 31

Chicken Cordon Bleu 73 *or* Better-for-You Meat Sauce with Pasta 90 *or* Shrimp and
Grits 100

Chocolate Cheesecake Cupcakes 156 *or* Raspberry Lemon Tea Cake 160 *or*
Brown Butter Cobbler 163

BREAKFAST FOR DINNER

"Blintz" Pancakes with Blueberry Syrup 25

Stuffed Egg White Omelet 38

Asparagus and Goat Cheese Quiche 29 *or* Chilaquiles 21

French Toast Bread Pudding 27

SUNDAY NIGHT SUPPER

Fish and Chips 111 *or* Chicken Cordon Bleu 73

Creamed Spinach 133

Chocolate Cheesecake Cupcakes 156

BUSY WEEKNIGHT DINNER

Pasta with Sausage and Cherry Tomatoes 97

Chopped "Taco" Salad 137

Chocolate Espresso Cookies 159

EXOTIC SPICES

Carrot Soup with a Kick 123

Flank Steak with Indian Salsa 79

Dessert Pizza (add a pinch of cardamom to the filling) 150

ITALIAN

White Pizza with Roasted Mushrooms 63

Better-for-You Meat Sauce with Pasta 90 *or* Chicken Meatballs 83

Panna Cotta 170 *or* Tiramisù 165

SOUTHERN CLASSICS

Cheese Biscuits 31

Shrimp and Grits 100

Brown Butter Cobbler 163

GAME NIGHT

Spicy Mary 41

Hot Wings 57

Seven-Layer Dip 67

Pizza with Sweet Peppers and Goat Cheese 65

Creamy Corn Chowder 140 *or* Quick Jambalaya 113

Super Fast and Easy

BREAKFAST ON THE RUN

Breakfast Burrito 19

Low-Fat Granola Bar 37

Violet Morning Smoothie 34 *or* Almondy Joy 36

LAST-MINUTE GET-TOGETHER / UNEXPECTED GUESTS

Spinach Dip 48

Sautéed Corn Cakes with Smoked Salmon 59

Asian Chicken Salad 77

Pineapple Mojitos 61

FIESTA

Pork Tacos 75

Chopped "Taco" Salad 137

Chocolate Volcano Cakes 147 (add a pinch of cinnamon and cayenne to the
    whipped cream)

EASIER ITALIAN

Roasted Chickpeas with Rosemary 53

Swordfish Arrabiata 107 *or* Cod Saltimbocca 102

Mocha Mousse 166

Index

Swordfish
    Fish Kebabs with Roasted Red
      Pepper Sauce, 108–9
    Swordfish Arrabiata, 107

T

Tacos, Pork, 75–76
"Taco" Salad, Chopped, 137
Tiramisù, 165
Tomatoes
    Chicken Meatballs, 83
    Eggs Italian Style, 22
    Pasta with Sausage and Cherry
      Tomatoes, 97
    Quick Jambalaya, 113
    Swordfish Arrabiata, 107
Turkey
    Quick Jambalaya, 113

Turkey Meatloaf with Dried
    Cranberries, 88–89

V

Vanilla Cherry Rice Pudding,
    149
Vegetable and Lentil Soup,
    Hearty, 125
Vegetables, 9–10
Violet Morning Smoothie, 34

W

White Chocolate Delight,
    152
White Pizza with Roasted
    Mushrooms, 63–64

© Evan Sung

Lauren Deen is a multiple Emmy Award–winning lifestyle producer and director for Martha Stewart, Bobby Flay, Food Network, *Food & Wine*, Walmart, and Condé Nast. She is also the co-executive producer of *Cook Yourself Thin* (Tiger Aspect/IMG/Lifetime Television).

Lauren is the author of *Kitchen Playdates* (Chronicle 2007) and the co-author of the *New York Times* bestseller *Cook Yourself Thin.*

A Blue-Ribbon graduate of Peter Kump's New York Cooking School (now ICE), Lauren lives in Brooklyn with her husband and two young children.